BOARDROOM BASICS:
A Pocket Guide
For Directors

by:

Roger H. Ford, Ph.D.

BEAR MOUNTAIN BOOKS
HARRISONBURG, VIRGINIA
1998

BOARDROOM BASICS:
A Pocket Guide For Directors

PRINTING HISTORY
First Edition - 1998
Second Printing - 1999

ISBN 0-9660372-0-0

Library of Congress Catalog Card Number
97-94364

All Rights Reserved
Copyright 1998 Roger H. Ford
This book may not be reproduced in any form without permission. For information, address: Bear Mountain Books, 211 East Grattan Street, Harrisonburg, Virginia 22801

Printed in the United States of America

*This book is dedicated to
Holly, Cassandra and Ryan
who give my life joy.*

Table of Contents

Forward **9**
John M. Nash, President of the National Association of Corporate Directors

Preface **11**

Acknowledgments **13**

1. INTRODUCTION **15**
- What Is A Private Company? 17
- Not All In The Family:
  A Role For Boards Of Private Companies 21

2. BOARD BUILDING BASICS **27**
- A Question Of Timing:
  When Do You Start Building Your Board? ... 29
- Building Your Board:
  Step One - Setting Objectives 35
- Building Your Board:
  Step Two - Board Composition 41
- Director Qualifications:
  The Owner's Perspective (Part One) 47
- Director Qualifications:
  The Owner's Perspective (Part Two) 55

3. THE DIRECTOR'S CORNER 65
- Just for Directors:
  What's In It For You? 67
- How To Be An Effective Director 75

4. THE BOARD IN ACTION:
Success And Failure
In The Boardroom Battlefield 87
- Battle Of The Boards:
  Tyson vs. WLR Foods 89
- Relinquishing The Helm
  Warren L. Braun, P.E. 97
- "All The Tire Tracks Stopped Here"–
  A Leader's Lesson
  Stanley C. Vance, Ph.D. 105

5. SPECIAL CASES:
Start-Up, Family And
International Boards 111
- The Role Of The Board
  During Start-Up 113
- Boards Of Directors And
  The Family-Owned Business 123
- Dispatch From Hanoi:
  Creating A Board Of Directors In The
  Socialist Republic Of Vietnam 131

- Vietnam Update:
  The Ben Tre Coconut Project Board
  Six Months Later 141

6. THE BOTTOM LINE:
Evaluating The CEO Of
The Private Company 149

- Evaluating The CEO-Owner (Part One)
  Process And Criteria 151
- Evaluating The CEO-Owner (Part Two)
  Who Should Do The Job? 159
- Evaluating The CEO-Owner (Part Three)
  How To Minimize The
  Impact Of Politics 163

7. SUMMARY 167

Biographies Of Contributing Authors
And Co-Authors 169

References 173

Foreword

John M. Nash
President
National Association of Corporate Directors
December 1997

In 1997, the National Association of Corporate Directors celebrated its first 20 years of corporate governance leadership. Our earliest members were primarily chief executives and directors from smaller firms, both public and private. By the early 1990s, our Association had grown to include a great number of directors serving on the boards of very large publicly held companies.

This book is a worthwhile addition to its field. I recommend it to all directors.

The increasing presence of directors from large public companies had a predictable impact on the editorial content of our publications, including *Director's Monthly,* our official newsletter. *DM* pages increasingly featured the people and issues associated with the *Fortune* 500. This was fine for directors of large companies, but it was less useful for directors of private companies—and they told us so in membership surveys.

So as the mid-decade approached, we faced a classic governance dilemma: How could we serve *all* our constituencies? The solution was clear. We would continue to cover large company issues, but would invite a well-known authority to write a regular column on the special issues facing directors of private companies.

First on our list was Professor Roger Ford and we were delighted when he agreed to write for *DM*. Fortunately for us, he was more than ready. In fact, he had been planning to approach us with the same idea and even had his first column in mind! Since then, his articles have come in like clockwork and have helped our members keep up to date with the changing issues facing private companies today.

Writing this forward gives me the opportunity to say publicly what I have often thought privately: Thank you for an excellent column, Roger Ford.

As the *summa* of all Ford columns, this book is a worthwhile addition to its field. I heartily recommend it to all directors.

Preface

Roger H. Ford, Ph.D.
Zane Showker Professor of Entrepreneurship
James Madison University
Harrisonburg, Virginia

I am pleased to offer this book to the growing body of literature supporting the world of corporate boards of directors. This book is the outgrowth of several years of my work as the Private Boards column editor of *Director's Monthly*, the official publication of the National Association of Corporate Directors. The column was aimed at helping the owners and directors of privately-owned companies better utilize the potential power of the board of directors. This book, based largely on updated versions of those columns, is designed to help the reader get started. It contains the basic concepts and tools needed to create and improve the private company board.

> **These are basic concepts and tools needed to create and improve the company board.**

Having worked in this field for 20 years as both academic and practitioner, I am thoroughly convinced that most private companies can benefit greatly from an effective board of directors. The main determining factor as to whether or not a private company *will* receive the benefits of a board is the attitude and determination of that company's owner or ownership team. To the millions of private company owners in the United States, I give this challenge: A good board may be the best investment you ever made for your business. The decision is yours. The ball is in your court.

Harvard's C. Roland Christensen once said that outside directors are the most under-appreciated and under-utilized asset available to any business. I agree with Professor Christensen, but more importantly, I think *it is the board as a unit that is the real key*. This unit should include both outside directors and inside directors combined with the owner/manager. A good board is an effective team—even if that team is small with, perhaps, only three or four members.

> **A good board may be the best investment you ever made for your business.**

It takes a lot of time and hard work to build any team, especially a high-level team like a board of directors, so let's get started now! I hope *Boardroom Basics* will help owners, managers, and directors of America's private companies begin the journey toward building effective boards of directors.

Acknowledgments

I am deeply indebted to those who helped bring this project together. First, I must acknowledge all those who helped with the creation of my previous book, "Outside Directors and the Privately Owned Firm," (1992, Quorum Books). From family, to professors at Syracuse University, to hundreds of *Inc.* 500 company presidents and board members, I am deeply in your debt. They have been individually acknowledged in that book.

Also, I would like to thank all those who provided critical comments on my research, as well as feedback on dozens of articles I have written regarding boards. These comments helped to generate ideas for the Private Boards Column in *Director's Monthly*. I especially think about all the directors, Chief Executive Officers, and others who have participated in my seminars, workshops and consultations, who often have taught me far more about boards than I was able to teach them.

Next, I wish to acknowledge my colleagues and others who have contributed to this book as authors or co-authors. I consider myself very fortunate to have worked at James Madison University since 1985. JMU is truly a great place to work, and I am surrounded by many outstanding colleagues, several of whom have works in this book. Each contributor is acknowledged in the introduction section of the appropriate chapter, and biographies appear at the end of the book.

Also, I sincerely thank Dr. Alexandra Reed Lajoux, Editor of *Director's Monthly*. Her encouragement and cheerleading, more than anything else, is responsible for the creation of the Private Boards column. Her careful and insightful editing has resulted in making many of my columns much more readable and interesting than they would have been without her help.

I am very grateful to Dana Patterson for editing and Barbara Sweatt for page layouts. Thank you also to Shaun College for cover art and to Timothy A. Heydon for logo design. This team really made Boardroom Basics a reality.

Finally, I thank God for giving me the opportunity and ability to work in such an exciting field where I am able (hopefully) to help entrepreneurs, directors and other company leaders. They are the real American entrepreneurs; men and women who are out there in the front lines every day trying to improve our economy and society by their hard work and leadership. Their success ultimately benefits us all.

— Roger H. Ford, Ph.D.
January, 1998

Chapter One:
INTRODUCTION

Owners of private companies typically have the freedom to choose whether to utilize a board of directors. A large percentage choose not to use them. These owners have not yet been persuaded that the effort and expense of building a board will pay off in terms of net benefit. The first article was written to help convince those reluctant company owners that the benefits of an effective board are, indeed, worth the cost. This point is made clearer by observing three actual case histories.

What Is A Private Company?

Roger H. Ford, Ph.D.
Zane Showker Professor of Entrepreneurship
James Madison University
Harrisonburg, Virginia

It is often said that America is a nation of small business, and that is certainly true. But it is equally true that America is a nation of private companies.

Small business can be defined in a number of ways, such as firms with 500 or fewer employees (the government's definition), or less than a certain dollar volume in sales (say, under $10 million or $100 million, depending on your preference).

Concentration of power makes private companies vastly different from their publicly traded counterparts.

The term "private companies" also begs definition. State and federal securities laws define public offerings (and therefore public companies); "private" companies are all enterprises that lie outside the normal reach of those laws.

When I refer to private companies, I am referring to firms with a high concentration of ownership. These are owned by one or a few individuals who have the power to make virtually any decision concerning those businesses. Many, but not all, of these companies are family businesses.

Concentration of power makes these firms vastly different from their publicly traded counterparts. It allows the owner/manager to be more flexible and move faster than other managers who must negotiate a maze of approvals before acting on many initiatives. But smaller private firms also face many problems, such as limited staff, absence of scale economies, oppressive government regulations, disproportionate tax burdens and reduced access to capital.

Private companies dominate our economy. Current estimates indicate that there are approximately 22 million businesses in the United States, and all but about 14,000 are privately owned. (Even about one-third of the *Fortune* 500 ranked firms are influenced by a family unit with a controlling interest of stock ownership.) While the public firms continue to reduce jobs through downsizing, rightsizing, re-engineering and just plain layoffs, private firms are continuing to grow in terms of numbers of firms, new jobs, sales growth and innovation.

This last point deserves attention. Scientific studies have shown that, in spite of their lack of resources, firms with fewer than 500 employees bring new innovations to the market almost 30 percent faster than larger businesses. Studies have also demonstrated that over 50 percent of the innovations in the United States come from small business. Small business, however, spends less than five percent of the nation's total corporate research budget!

We should all agree on how vital smaller private companies are to our economy. As the nation's smaller private businesses go, so goes the rest of our economy. Therefore, any tool which can strengthen our private firms should be thoroughly studied. The board of directors is an excellent place to begin.

— *Director's Monthly, Vol. 18, No. 1, January 1994*

Not All In The Family:
A Role For Boards Of Private Companies

Roger H. Ford, Ph.D.
Zane Showker Professor of Entrepreneurship
James Madison University
Harrisonburg, Virginia

An increasing number of private companies are discovering the benefits of a solid working board of directors. How do boards for private firms differ from boards of public firms, and how can they help improve the performance of the smaller family-owned firm?

Difference

In the private firm the manager is typically also the owner, and can therefore fire a director or the entire board on a moment's notice!

There is a simple but profoundly significant difference in the boards of public versus private firms. This is a difference of power. In large, publicly traded firms, the board is required by law and empowered by the shareholders, who concentrate their dispersed ownership in the annual ritual of electing directors.

This involvement of non-management owners in the board selection process gives the directors of public companies a degree of independence not enjoyed by directors of private companies. In the private firm, the manager is typically also the owner, and can therefore fire a director or the entire board on a moment's notice! The owners of private companies will establish and use boards only if they believe that their firms will receive a net benefit for the effort and investment required to set up and maintain them.

What are the facts? Are private firms taking full advantage of their boards? Well, not as many are as probably should be, but recent statistics indicate that the use of the board by private firms is catching on. In my study of *Inc.* 500 firms, I found that about one-third of these successful private companies have no boards, one-third only have a nominal board of insiders, and one-third have a working board of some type with one or more outsiders participating. One out of three is not bad, considering the rarity of working boards in the past.

Three Cases

But not all of these firms with working boards are getting all they can out of them. Take the case of a Richmond area service firm that got rid of all its outsiders a few years ago. The owner/manager and president of this rapidly growing company felt that the board needed to meet so frequently, and usually on such short notice, that he terminated the outsiders to avoid the ritual of having "waiver of 30 day notice of meeting" forms prepared and signed, and to eliminate the frustration on all sides caused by poor outsider attendance. Yet the firm benefited greatly from the outsiders when they were used, and their expertise and connections, particularly in the area of raising capital, were sorely missed later.

So what happened here? Assuming the owner/manager is an intelligent rational person (which I believe he is) there must be a reason why he eliminated a resource that was so valuable to him. He obviously concluded that the *net* cost of using the outsiders was greater than the *net* contribution they made in his situation.

Presidents of private companies need to be open to learning to use boards for maximum effectiveness.

Could this have been changed? I think the answer is yes, with patience and time. Presidents of private companies need to be open to learning how to use their boards for maximum effectiveness, and to making the investment to build their boards into stronger management tools.

Let's consider another example. A small manufacturing firm with too little capital and too few customers was struggling to survive and grow out of its infancy. During its first year, the firm organized a working board comprised of a mix of both inside and outside directors. As the company approached its fifth year, severe financial problems developed. The combination of start-up expenses, slower than desired sales growth and accounts receivables past 90 days had the company near insolvency. A promised bank loan backed by the Small Business Administration loan guarantee was the only solution in sight.

Everything seemed to be solved, but then nothing happened. The bank had been told by the Small Business Administration that the deal would be approved quickly. Three months later the wheels of government bureaucracy were still stuck. Fortunately, an outside director came to the rescue. Using his personal contacts with elected officials, including a mayor and a congressman, the director was able to prod Small Business Administration officials to move the mountain of paperwork and expedite the loan guarantee paperwork.

The manufacturer finally got its money just days after several key suppliers began demanding cash-on-delivery payment—a condition that would have been impossible for the company to meet, according to the officers. "If the bottleneck had lasted one week longer we would have been out of business," said an outsider on the board.

Another small manufacturing company[1] found a sudden use for its board of directors when the young son and

---

[1]*This case, and many others, are detailed in my earlier book, "Boards of Directors and the Privately Owned Firm," (1992), Quorum Books.*

star who had been running the business died unexpectedly in a plane crash.

The board appointed a qualified family member to manage the succession process. This manager selected a less qualified family member to head the company. This decision led to employee dissatisfaction and a decline in performance. An outside director convinced the more qualified family member to add a venture capitalist to the board. As an active investor, the venture capitalist eventually came to serve as the Chief Executive Officer, and company performance recovered—to the delight of family members, who retained ownership control throughout the process.

Private firms that establish working boards of directors and use them effectively find them to be instrumental in assisting management in countless ways.

The Good News

I could go on with dozens of similar stories. Private firms that establish working boards of directors and use them effectively find them to be instrumental in assisting management in countless ways. A board can be a surrogate for internal talent and other resources that smaller firms simply do not always have. That is not to say that every firm not using a board is making a mistake. In fact, I know of many private companies—particularly smaller ones—with no board who manage just fine.

Yet it is clear to me that any firm without a working board is missing out on an opportunity that might someday make a critical difference. Whether the issue is raising money, cutting through government red tape, finding a successor when the president dies suddenly or any number of other issues, the board can be a powerful tool for private firms.

— *Director's Monthly, Vol. 18, No. 1, January 1994*

Chapter Two:
BOARD-BUILDING BASICS

Being persuaded, of course, is only the first step. Next comes the hard work of putting a board together and making it work. This takes much time, energy and expense. Naturally, the work of running the day-to-day business will not stop to allow the owner/manager to devote full time to this task. Therefore, it helps to have some guidelines to make the job easier. Fortunately, there are many success stories out there, so one does not have to completely reinvent the board-wheel. By following some of the ideas in this chapter, much time and effort can be saved. This will help you get your board up and running faster.

The five articles in this chapter deal with some of the most fundamental issues of board development: timing, i.e., when to build the board, board objectives, board composition and director qualifications. By carefully considering these issues before getting started, many common problems typical of private company boards can be minimized or even avoided altogether.

A Question of Timing:
When Do You Start Building Your Board?

Roger H. Ford, Ph.D
Zane Showker Professor of Entrepreneurship
James Madison University
Harrisonburg, Virginia

If you agree that the board is a good idea, exactly when should you begin to build it? Well, that depends on your goals as the private company owner. Outsiders and theorists may clearly see what a board can do, but this does not guarantee that the entrepreneur or leader will know when to act!

> **The sooner you build your board the better, say experienced observers. Why not start today?**

Let's briefly consider three cases presented later in Chapter 4. In Dr. Braun's ComSonics case, he could not have successfully transferred the control of his firm to the employees unless he had a capable board that could assist with the transference of power and provide stability of leadership into the new era of the business's leadership. In Dr. Vance's Seiberling Rubber case, the absence of a board prevented management from dealing with a takeover situation more effectively. Both cases clearly demonstrate that the best time to build a strong and effective board is *before* you need it! Braun's article demonstrates this with a positive case, and Vance's article with a negative one.

In rural Virginia, another case where a strong board helped to protect an independent company occurred in the unsuccessful and highly publicized takeover attempt of Virginia-based WLR Foods by Arkansas raider Don Tyson of Tyson Foods. The published accounts suggested that powerful and well-connected poultry king Tyson would easily buy out the less experienced WLR Foods. The markets apparently agreed, reacting as if Tyson had won as soon as his intentions were announced. WLR's management and board, however, had other ideas, and pulled off a brilliant defensive strategy by aggressively acting to thwart Tyson at every play. As I followed this case in local, national and international news, I noticed that WLR board members were engaged in this action every step of the way. If WLR had needed to recruit and train its board *after* Tyson announced

Some typical reasons for developing boards:
- **window dressing (public relations)**
- **stockholder/stakeholder involvement**
- **networking (access to markets, etc.)**
- **strategy, long-range planning**
- **independent assessment/review/audit**
- **specialized expertise**
- **innovation/new ventures**
- **arbitration (family, partner feuds)**
- **management continuity and succession,**
- **crisis management**

his takeover plans, it would have already been too late for WLR to act.

The point here is that the issue of timing in board planning and building relates to the objectives for which the board is desired. The owners of private companies are usually under no compulsion to have and utilize a board unless they want to. So the question of timing relates directly to what the company's owner-founder (or successor) wants the board to do. Some typical reasons private companies cite for developing boards include:

- window dressing (public relations)
- stockholder/stakeholder involvement
- networking (access to markets, etc.)
- strategy, long-range planning
- independent assessment/review/audit
- specialized expertise
- innovation/new ventures
- arbitration (family, partner feuds)
- management continuity and succession, and
- crisis management.

For example, let's take the objective window dressing. This is a common objective in initial public offerings and private placements, when the goal is to place a couple of well-known names on a prospectus to enhance stock sales. This can be accomplished fairly easily and quickly and can be an effective marketing ploy. Many investors do not understand the role of the board, and name recognition may be a factor regardless of what the director may or may not contribute to corporate governance. Or, let's look at the objectives of independent assessment and arbitration. One can easily imagine recruiting a key outsider who could provide some types of contributions to board meetings and to the company's governance process fairly quickly. Therefore, we can see that there are some objectives that can be met with little advance planning regarding when the board must be developed or strengthened.

However, when we look at this list of possible board objectives (and realize that it is certainly incomplete), we must notice that the more critical objectives, such as dealing with crises and succession planning, cannot be accomplished unless the board is already in place. A competent board cannot be created like an instant cake mix ("Just add water and stir"). A good board is more like a professional sports team, even the best players are ineffective on the playing field without hours of practice and real game experience, which can take years.

Many strong-willed entrepreneurs will have a hard time accepting that they may need a board for heavy-duty issues such as succession planning. They would prefer to pretend that they are going to live forever and not worry about such negative things. The reality of all businesses is, of course, that they all must deal with serious matters and even crises eventually. The positioning of even one top-notch director can then make a tremendous difference.

Case In Point

A few years ago, I was asked to consult for the board of a large family-owned firm that was just one of about 20 firms controlled by this family group. This dynamic enterprise was suddenly found in the estate of a roaring entrepreneur who had died suddenly and unexpectedly. Although the board was not operating ideally by anyone's standards, it had at least had one major asset—a single, key outside director who could see the business (and most of the overall estate) from the top level.

The positioning of even one top-notch director can make a tremendous difference.

This director sized up the family members and other non-family managers and quickly suspected that they were not capable of keeping the business and related enterprises going alone. He invited me to help evaluate the situation. Together we developed a plan to recruit an outside, caretaker CEO while the family members matured in their ability to eventually resume leadership of the firm. I worked with the outsider and others until the leadership crisis was

Boardroom Basics

over. Today, the outside director remains active as a stabilizing force representing continuity between the old, transitional and future leaders.

I am convinced that without the presence of this one director, the new generation would have attempted to take over prematurely, and the results for this multimillion dollar family enterprise could have been disastrous.

So what is the bottom line about the timing of building a board? Well, for many board objectives, timing can sometimes wait until management feels that the need is obvious. However, for more vital issues, such as providing for unplanned succession, or dealing with a crisis, the bottom line is that it is never too early to begin building your board, and in some cases, it would already be too late.

— *Director's Monthly, Vol. 18, No. 11, November 1994*

Building Your Board:
Step One—Setting Objectives

Roger H. Ford, Ph.D.
Zane Showker Professor of Entrepreneurship
James Madison University
Harrisonburg, Virginia

I have frequently made the point that private company boards are different from public company boards and that this difference is largely one of power. The owner of a private firm typically will have and use a board of directors only if he or she believes a net benefit will result. That is, the owner believes that the board will generate more in benefits than the costs (time, expense and administrative headaches, etc.) necessary to achieve those benefits. In effect, the presence (or absence) of boards in private companies is much more a function of the free marketplace than in the case of public companies, where shareholders, industry regulations, government controls, big union pressures and other political forces all contribute to create and perpetuate boards.

Before building your board, plan it!

The entrepreneurial owner can often create a board simply because he believes it is good for the business, while his big business manager counterpart typically "inherits" a ready-made board passed on throughout the ages to successive managers.

Getting Started

So how does the owner/manager get started? As always, one must begin with objectives and goals. Private companies use boards for many purposes and not all of these purposes are appropriate for every firm. For example, private firms often use their boards to assist with company strategy and policies, raise capital, provide independent audit or review and ensure managerial continuity during succession. Other common objectives of private boards are to provide specialized expertise, serve as a sounding board, arbitrate between feuding family members or partners or simply to serve as window dressing to impress the bankers. So then, the very first step in creating (or re-energizing) a board is to set its basic objectives, that is, to establish exactly what the owner/manager hopes to accomplish by using the board.

Great Expectations

I once spent a day interviewing a company owner and several board members of a service firm located in Richmond, Virginia. After some time had passed in casual conversations, I realized that I could not tell what the board was trying to do. The entire group seemed very disorganized and unsure of itself. I finally asked the owner (as diplomatically as I could) exactly what motivated him to create his board. He replied that he had read an article in *The Wall Street Journal* that said every small company needed a board, so he started one. I asked him what he hoped to accomplish with the board and he confessed that he did not really know. Unfortunately, all the board seemed to accomplish was to waste a good deal of time and resources, while frustrating everyone involved. Without leadership and direction from the top, the board forum was virtually useless. Fortunately, after going over a list of options very much like the ones listed in this chapter, the owner realized what he really wanted and proceeded to achieve it.

> **Without leadership and direction from the top, the board forum [is] virtually useless.**

Many company owners quickly become disappointed with their boards when they realize they are not producing results. This disappointment can usually be traced to vague or overly optimistic expectations, setting up a board with no goals or with unrealistic goals beyond reach for a board, at least in the short term. The owner realizes that the board is little more than an expensive "rap session." Lots of talk, but little to show for it. This was certainly the case of the Richmond firm mentioned above.

Boardroom Basics

It was also the case with a CEO who disbanded his board, which included several outsiders, because it was slow to the point of being sluggish, "like a Congress." He added that he "had to spend too much time explaining things to them to justify the support they were able to give me." In this case, the CEO had set objectives for the board that were simply not obtainable quickly enough (if ever!) to satisfy the impatience of an entrepreneurial business owner.

Generic Board Types

Window dressing. Primarily enhance the image and prestige of the firm.

Strategic. Deals with long-term and policy-related issues of the firm.

Operational. Directors are involved in a wide variety of routine and day-to-day activities of the firm.

Networking. Create and/or enhance the firm's linkages to the outside world through the personal contacts of the outside directors.

All-purpose. Involved in all levels of the firm's activities to some extent.

Five Categories

Based on my experiences with private companies, most boards fall into five basic categories. These categories, which I call generic board types, do not suggest different types of boards you can choose, but, rather, help explain the primary purposes or functions of boards of directors. These types are:

Window dressing. These boards exist primarily to enhance the image and prestige of the firm. Director duties are largely ceremonial.

Strategic. This type of board deals with a variety of long-term and policy-related issues of the firm. The board's role may be either advisory or decision-making.

Operational. In this kind of board, directors are involved in a wide variety of routine and day-to-day activities of the firm. It is typically composed of mostly inside directors.

Networking. These boards are established to create and/or enhance the firm's external linkages to the outside world through the personal contacts of the outside directors.

All-purpose. This hybrid of all the other types is involved in all levels of the firm's activities to some extent. This type may be the ultimate goal for many private companies, but it is difficult to create from scratch. It requires much time and commitment to achieve.

The main point here is to recognize that it takes time to create an effective board, so the objectives chosen need to be reasonable and appropriate.

The main point here is to recognize that it takes time to create an effective board, so the objectives chosen need to be reasonable and appropriate, given the needs of the firm. Most firms should start with a few objectives, and use the board for more activities as the group matures into a strong body. A board of directors is a tool, and as with any new tool, it takes time and practice to become proficient. Individual directors need time to learn their roles, and the board as a group needs to learn how to work as a team.

Bottom Line

The bottom line is that in order to build an effective board, you must first start out with a reasonable set of objectives. Next, you need to staff the board with the talent required to reach those objectives, which is the topic of the next article.

— *Director's Monthly, Vol. 18, No. 3, March 1994*

Building Your Board:
Step Two—Board Composition

Roger H. Ford, Ph.D.
Zane Showker Professor of Entrepreneurship
James Madison University
Harrisonburg, Virginia

In the last article, I discussed various objectives a private firm may set for establishing a working board of directors. Now we will build upon this foundation and look at board composition. Keep in mind, however, that the way the board is staffed must be subordinate to the objectives set for the board. That is, boards (or, if there is no board yet, managers) must recruit directors who have the talent and ability to help the board reach its objectives.

The first step in recruiting board members is to decide exactly what you want them to do!

So the first step in recruiting board members is to decide exactly what you want them to do. Otherwise you may wind up with directors who are not qualified for the job they are assigned.

Whole Team Concept

The next step is to begin thinking about your board with a "whole team" concept. Recruiting a board is a little different from recruiting employees. When you hire a new bookkeeper, for example, your primary focus will be on the candidate's ability to do one specific job. With a board, however, you are trying to build a team, where the total package is more important than a single person's skill or prestige.

In contemplating the process of board-building, I like to use the mental picture of a pie. Think of a hole in the shape of a pie. The hole represents the total objectives you can imagine for the board to address. Then think of potential directors as being pie-shaped slices placed inside the hole. Not all slices (potential directors) are the same size, or even the same shape. One outstanding director may fill up half the pie plate, whereas it may take four or five petite slices (less qualified potential directors) to fill up the other half.

This exercise helps managers or boards avoid making premature commitments to any single director until they have considered how that individual would affect the total composition of the board as a team. It also helps to keep the board down to an easily manageable size (typically five to seven for new boards) since the larger the group, the more difficult scheduling, communications and board management becomes.

Building Your Board: Step Two

Examples

Let's look at a couple of real examples where the failure to set goals before recruiting directors hurt the effectiveness of boards and the firms they serve. One case involved the premature recruiting of a director who was selected for his financial expertise. The director was genuinely interested and talented in financial forecasting and analysis, areas where this engineering-oriented firm was weak. He was also a friend of the leadership team. This made it easy to ask him to come on board. Indeed, he was the first director recruited. The only problem was that he lived about 150 miles away and was unable to come to the firm more than two or three times per year for formal board meetings. Recruiting this individual turned out to be a mistake, since he just wasn't available often enough to meet the needs of the firm. It would have been easy to find similar experts who lived closer. However, the firm's managers lived with this situation for three years. They were trapped because:

> **Avoid making premature commitments to any single director [before considering] how that individual would affect the total composition of the board as a team.**

1) They really liked the man and found his insight useful when it was available, so they did not want to ask him to resign.

2) Also, since he knew he was recruited for financial

expertise, they did not feel right about bringing on another financial expert as a board member for fear of hurting his feelings.
3) Finally, they felt that even if they did bring on another financial expert, the board would get too big.

Another example concerns a firm whose directors were expected to help sell a significant amount of stock in addition to several other board duties. A problem arose when the firm realized that the group of directors chosen, while excellent with respect to many other board objectives, did not have the necessary connections to reach the stock sale goal. To address the problem, additional directors were recruited to help meet this objective. However, the final board composition was far too large. In hindsight, some of the directors chosen earlier turned out to be expendable, or at least not as valuable as initially hoped.

Both problems addressed in these examples could have been avoided had the firm's leaders thought more deeply about their board's total composition prior to recruiting and selecting individual directors.

Other Issues

Of course, that is not all there is to recruiting and developing the board team. One must look at many other issues, including the individual qualifications of each director and how the personalities of the directors will work together and with management. But always begin by considering the objectives the board is expected to accomplish and then what the total board composition needs to look like in order to best address those objectives.

— *Director's Monthly, Vol. 18, No. 5, May 1994*

Director Qualifications:
Part One—The Owner's Perspective

Roger H. Ford, Ph.D.
Zane Showker Professor of Entrepreneurship
James Madison University
Harrisonburg, Virginia

The average private company owner mostly wants a board that can protect and improve his wealth by overseeing and assisting the performance of management. Therefore, the recruitment and selection of the right directors, either outsiders or insiders, is of paramount importance to owners.

While no generalities can tell the complete story, I would like to offer

> **If these criteria sound too rigid...just consider the question, "Who would you want to look after your entire net worth?"**

some basic criteria that I consider (with only occasional exception) to be the minimum qualifications for board membership in a private company. If these criteria sound too rigid, subjective or picky, just consider the question, "Who would you want to look after your entire net worth?" which is the case with the vast majority of privately owned companies.

In order to get it out of the way, let's start with what is probably the most controversial of all my criteria.

Age

Every lawyer should know that the minimum legal age requirement for directors ranges from 18 to 21, depending on the various state laws. However, being legally qualified to serve on a board has no association whatsoever with being qualified in terms of intelligence, maturity and experience. For a number of reasons, I believe 30 is a reasonable age to begin directing. I have made this point hundreds of times in consulting and lectures, and I have never had a single person verbally disagree with me, although I will keep my mind open for anyone who cares to write to me with a strong counterargument.

There is something about turning 30 that seems to signal that one is now an adult. Maybe it is a carryover from Biblical traditions that a man is not a man until that age. Maybe it is the fact that most people 30 or older have married, had children, bought cars and a house or two and have switched jobs, been promoted, or even fired. Such events seem to wisen us up. Whatever the cause, it is my observation, both from my own life and board experiences, and from what I have learned from others, that directors under the age of "thirtysomething" are just not effective.

I will offer two exceptions. The first is for family firms where there is a strong need to quickly acclimate a young potential successor in top leadership. This may be the case

Director Qualifications: Part One

where a company founder is experiencing poor health or the firm is going through changes that necessitate next generation involvement at the helm quickly.

Do not interpret this exception too loosely, however. In several cases where I have seen this exception in practice, the "urgency" was little more than vanity or ego on the part of the senior or junior generation—or both!

The second exception is in the case where the firm is involved in a particular industry that is heavily dependent on youth culture. Fashion, music, TV, etc. come to mind. Still, one can argue that in these cases what is really needed are more youthful consultants, not directors.

A final point about age. Age is much more mental than biological. Some 30-year-olds, and even 20-year-olds demonstrate more maturity than some "sixtysomethings." Some older directors need to be replaced when their thinking becomes too rigid or old-fashioned. What is really needed are directors with the maturity and experience of adults who have not yet "retired" mentally. Some senior citizens can still contribute effectively to the board at 80 or even 90. Others should be retired at 55 or never asked to serve at all!

> **Age is much more mental than biological... What is really needed are directors with the maturity & experience of adults.**

Character

This next point is a little touchy in light of the "politically correct" movement which began in the 1990s. Needless to say, a reputation of good character and high integrity is essential for any board member. Unfortunately, obtaining reliable information and truthful references about a person's character is proving to be very difficult. Personnel directors and general managers alike are becoming increasingly frustrated with the difficulty in learning the truth about people until often it is too late. This is unfortunate. A good company image can take years to build, but it can be destroyed overnight by association with unethical characters at the corporate governance level.

There are many methods of background investigation, including membership checking, employment history and, in some cases, private investigations. Perhaps the best method is to seek the opinions of other persons who are mutually known by you and the potential board member nominee. Someone you know personally will be much more likely to give you a frank and honest opinion than a stranger who, in this day and age, may be more concerned about lawsuits than the needs of your company's board. Try especially to talk with individuals who have worked with your candidate in another board capacity, whether on a corporate, or even a nonprofit board. Churches and civic groups

Director Qualifications: Part One

such as the Rotary Club can also be helpful for basic background checks.

I will leave this point with two caveats. First, keep the character checking as quiet and discreet as possible. This will avoid embarrassing any of the parties involved, as well as reduce the likelihood of a nuisance lawsuit later. Second, never rely too securely on what you learn about someone's character. We have witnessed an explosion of cases of unethical, illegal and immoral behavior by persons otherwise held in high public esteem. The disclosures of such transgressions can seriously affect the institutions and/or organizations associated with the offending individual, regardless of whether the individual was an otherwise effective director or whether the "sin" had any direct effect on your business. I have seen many cases where some dark disclosure of a director's "secret sins" has resulted in a loss of customers, decline in employee morale and even a drop in stock value. Therefore, good character should never be assumed without some solid investigation.

> **A good company image can take years to build, but it can be destroyed overnight by association with unethical characters at the corporate governance level.**

Knowledge and Skills

Obviously, the knowledge and skills of a potential director matter enormously to owners forming their boards. It is very important to carefully match the abilities of a particular board candidate with those abilities needed by the board. What are the objectives of the company? What role does the board play in leading, governing, and/or advising the firm? What knowledge and skills do other members of the board already possess? What specific talent or abilities do they lack or need to strengthen?

I have previously suggested that it is helpful to build a board team using a pie metaphor. Consider what a whole pie looks like. It is complete and it contains more than one slice. But no two slices are exactly alike. Nor are any two pies cut exactly the same way. One pie may be cut into three big pieces, while another is cut into eight small ones.

Comparing this idea to boards, we can consider that there are many ways to slice up the board. Some boards may be complete with only three or four directors while some may have 12 or more. There is no magic number of people needed. It all depends on, among other things, the knowledge and skills that are being assembled, and how many people it will take to become as nearly complete a group as possible. Add to this logistical considerations such as coordinating, assembling and managing a smaller or larger group.

On one board, a single director may possess half the

knowledge and skill of the entire board, while two or three other directors may be more minor players. On another board, seven or eight members may more or less contribute equally to provide the skill and knowledge needed to make the board a harmonious whole.

It may be a useful exercise to develop a list of critical talents needed for the board, similar to a job description, and compare this list with each current or candidate board member to see how well they match up. This can reduce the chance that some directors will be recruited for the wrong reasons.

Next I will discuss three additional director qualifications and conclude with a final comment for company owners seeking to find "the ideal director."

— Director's Monthly, Vol. 19, No. 11, November 1995

Director Qualifications:
Part Two—The Owner's Perspective

Roger H. Ford, Ph.D.
Zane Showker Professor of Entrepreneurship
James Madison University
Harrisonburg, Virginia

Previously, I began a discussion of what I consider to be essential qualifications for directors of private boards. As I resume that discussion, it may be helpful to point out that the qualifications of private firm directors are different from those sought by publicly owned corporations in one important way: The public director must, in part, represent a larger public in a way that the private director does not. That is, the primary role of the private director is to serve the interests of a single owner or a small group of owners, since they own the firm outright. The public director has more of a sense of social responsibility since the ownership of the firm is widely distributed amongst perhaps thousands of individuals and institutional owners.

> **The primary role of the private director is to serve the interests of a single owner or a small group of owners.**

The private director protects *your* wealth (referring to company owners), whereas the public director protects *their* wealth (referring to a dispersed group of owners) while trying to balance the needs of business with the needs of other shareholders and the public at large.

Keeping this in mind, we can now continue to develop our list of director qualifications. In the previous article, we discussed three qualifications: age, character, knowledge and skills. We now will continue with three additional qualifications.

Interest

A key qualification for any board member is a sincere interest in the business itself. This may come as a shock to many entrepreneurs, but not everyone will love your business as much as you do! Yet, even with a total absence of interest, many prospective board members will gladly accept an invitation to serve. The reason for this may be that they are simply flattered at the invitation or that they do not want to hurt your feelings and cannot think of a polite way to say no. Then again, they may accept because it will look good on their resumes.

Let's face it, board memberships are prestigious—even for the smaller private company board. They are a sort of corporate status symbol that says "I've arrived" in the minds of many would-be directors.

It may take a little effort to distinguish between flattery or self-serving interest and genuine interest in the business under discussion. However, it is worth the trouble to determine the extent of interest of all nominees under consideration. Directors without real interest may attend a few meetings, but they will not be there when they are really needed. And they will not put in the effort required to be truly effective, even if they are good actors and play the part for a time. Directors of real value *will* "be there" for your company, whenever they can, and their presence will be a real force for progress.

The difference between the chaff and the wheat can become apparent during an effective interviewing process. Those not so interested will talk mainly about themselves and quickly change the topic of conversation from the needs of the firm to the talents of the proposed director. Candidates with real interest will ask questions about the firm. They will want to know all they can about the industry and the key players involved. They will ask about people and they will really listen to the answers—and maybe even take notes! There *is* a difference. Take time to discern it.

> **It is worth the trouble to determine the extent of interest of all nominees under consideration. Directors without real interest...will not be there when they are really needed.**

Time

It goes without saying that a board member who never

has time to attend meetings or other board functions will be of little value. Time availability is not the same thing as interest. Someone may be very interested in serving your board, but simply not have the time to be an effective director. In fact, one of the frequent complaints about outside directors that I learned from my study of *Inc.* 500 companies was that they were rarely available except for regularly scheduled board meetings, and even then they tended to miss a lot of meetings.

On the other hand, I tend to be a little suspicious of board candidates who do not have a full plate of activities and obligations. As the saying goes, "If you want to get something done, ask a busy person." The point is that good board candidates will be people who are already successful at other things. No one of this caliber has any *free* time. Rather, they will have to *make* time in order to serve on the board.

Fortunately, successful people typically possess excellent time management skills and are good at juggling many commitments on their calendars and in their minds at once. They regularly get things done much more effectively and efficiently than others.

Someone seriously considering an offer to serve will want to know exactly how much time board membership requires. This needs to be thought out in advance by the

Director Qualifications: Part Two

board leadership. How many meetings will be held, and how long will they last? What other duties will be expected of board members and what is the time commitment of each? These questions are healthy and indicate that the nominee is seriously considering the cost of serving on the board.

A specific long-range calendar of board meetings and activities is a very helpful way to help manage time pressures. But you should also be willing to refuse a board seat to anyone who is simply *too* busy, unless he or she is willing to shed commitments to rise to the occasion of service on your board.

A few years ago, I was asked to accept an appointment as a director

You should be willing to refuse a board seat to anyone who is simply *too* busy.

of a nonprofit organization whose mission was very important to me. I realized that it was a big commitment of time—more than most boards on which I have served. As I considered the cost of time involved, I realized I simply could not meet the expectations that the leadership had for me. Yet, I still wanted to accept.

After much consideration, I resolved the issue by getting out of some of my other obligations, including two other board positions (one term was about to come to an end anyway). I figured out how many hours the new board would require. I refused to give up any of the precious little family time I had, so I found the amount of time needed in other business and professional activities I was willing to give up.

I know of some directors with unbelievably busy schedules. Their activities keep them in a whirlwind of activity all over the world. Yet many of them are very effective directors. They attend most regularly scheduled meetings (even if by speaker phone) and are occasionally available for other functions. But they cannot be there all the time that the board management may need them. Management must deal with this trade-off. The better the board candidate (that is, the more talented, accomplished, etc.), the less he or she will probably be available. Make the decision with your eyes open and try to manage as best you can the time that you do get the director's attention.

No Conflict of Interest

Conflict of interest is one of those fuzzy concepts that people frequently cannot define. They say they know it when they see it. Unfortunately, many good and wise people will often disagree about individual cases where there appears to be conflict. Conflict is much more gray than simply not breaking any laws. Determining whether a director has a conflict of interest with respect to a particular board or issue requires a great deal of judgment and a strong sense of ethics. Even then, it is not always clear. This area is getting more and more complex every day as our economy becomes more global and multicultural. Perceptions of right and wrong and other personal codes of ethics and conduct are heavily influenced by culture, and the mixing of—as well as tensions between—cultures is happening at an ever-increasing rate of speed.

Rather than try to offer a complete formula for avoiding conflict, which I cannot do, I will offer some simple advice on how to avoid the obvious conflicts. As you are thinking about recruiting board members, certainly good networking and connections with the outside world are desirable. But avoid going over the edge where connections really become "co-optation."

> **Good networking and connections with the outside world are desirable. But avoid going over the edge where connections really become "co-optation."**

For example, if you need someone with financial expertise on the board, do not ask your own banker in an attempt to "influence" him to give you more favorable rates. If you need advice on obtaining government contracts, do not try to recruit an agency official who may have some say over who gets contracts. I realize that these things do happen every day, but it is not the route to building a healthy board or firm for the long term.

Interlocking directorships can often result in more efficient firms with many profitable advantages. But they can also lead to price-fixing and other illegal activities. Think about your motives when identifying board member candidates and try to avoid conflict situations early while you are still building your board.

Summary: The Ideal Director

While boardroom life would be much simpler if there were a standardized test for finding and qualifying directors, in reality, there is no such test. In my *Inc.* 500 study I asked both CEOs and board members for their opinions about what it takes to be a good director. I received a broad range of characteristics, totaling well over two dozen items. Several characteristics were mentioned frequently, such as specialized knowledge and expertise (corporate law, science and technology being the most common). Many other characteristics were considered critical by one or only a few respondents. Some of these included "creative," "risk taker," "Christian," and even one who stated a "willingness to serve without insurance!"

The point here is that we can never hope to find a single set of characteristics that would qualify each and every director for every board. There are too many variables to consider. Even if we could develop a perfect set of qualifications, probably every person on the planet would be disqualified somehow! Just use *some* set of criteria (mine here is a good start) and consider the impact of each director to the overall team. After all, it is the board as a *unit* that is the most important.

— *Director's Monthly, Vol. 20, No. 1, January 1996*

Chapter Three:
THE DIRECTOR'S CORNER

Although I frequently refer to the board as a tool, it is not a tool like a photocopier, laptop computer or telephone. That is, the board is not merely some machine ready to do its master's bidding at the push of a button. The board is a living entity, composed of living, breathing and hopefully highly competent, successful, and opinionated individuals. Unlike our digital- electro-mechanical machines, this machine (the board) will often talk back and challenge its master, which is, in part, exactly what is desired.

Therefore, the selection of directors, as discussed in the last chapter, is very important. But the feeding of directors is also of extreme importance. Just as a machine needs electricity, oil and proper maintenance, board members need to receive proper fuel and maintenance. The two articles which follow were written especially for directors. They help directors decide 1) if they really want the job of board member and 2) if they are being properly fed, maintained and utilized as directors. Also, these articles will help individual directors decide if they are truly rising to the challenge of directorship and if not, provide a basis for improved performance in the future.

Just for Directors:
What's In It For You?

Roger H. Ford, Ph.D.
Zane Showker Professor of Entrepreneurship
James Madison University
Harrisonburg, Virginia

I have a bias. I confess. Typically, I concentrate on providing information that the private board *leader* needs to build and maintain an effective board of directors. I make no apologies for that fact. However, in this chapter, I am going to take a different tack and provide special information just for *board members*.

Five benefits of serving on private company boards.

(Leaders, you are welcome to read this also. You may wish to borrow some of these ideas and give them to your board members at your next meeting.)

In the rush to persuade business owners to take advantage of the benefits of having an effective, working board of directors, we governance advocates often take it for granted that competent, committed board members are already on hand or available to serve once they are invited to join. While I believe this is generally true, it is a little easier said than done. Potential directors *are* available—lots of them—but they need to be convinced that board service, especially for private companies, is worth the effort. In other words, they need to know that board membership is not simply a one-way proposition where they give a great deal of their time and energy to the board and get nothing (except a headache) in return.

The purpose of this article is to provide a list of some of the more common benefits of serving as a board member, answering the question, "What's in it for you?" Although this list is certainly not complete, it does summarize the opinions of hundreds of board members whom I have interviewed about this question. Specifically, I often ask board members, particularly outsiders, the questions, "Why do you serve as a director? What do YOU get out of it?" I am sure that this list is not complete, but it does summarize the opinions of what I would consider "typical" directors of private company boards. Also, please note that the information comes "straight from the horses' (directors') mouths." That is, this is *not* a propaganda piece supplied by board leaders trying to recruit directors.

Experience

Probably the best answer to the "What's in it for you?" question is experience. Private board service allows outside directors to gain valuable corporate governance experience in a setting apart from where they spend the bulk of their working time. This view of another business "from the top" is priceless to most directors, who get to learn how other company leaders handle (or mishandle) the difficult long-range as well as day-to-day challenges of business leadership. This benefit of experience is often valued more by younger directors, but it is deeply appreciated by older, more experienced directors as well.

Prestige

While I personally would rather ignore this reason for private board service, I must mention it in all fairness, because I have learned that it is a major motivator for many who seek and accept directorships. Let's be perfectly honest. There is a certain mystique and attractiveness to serving on boards of directors. It is something akin to an exclusive club, a membership which implies, "I have arrived" into the elite business community. Since there are few board positions in the *Fortune* 500 and those are very difficult to acquire, private boards offer an attractive alternative for individuals who desire to be in hubs of business activity. For people who are already successful financially (and most qualified candidates should be), the prestige factor may be more impor-

> **Private board service allows outside directors to gain valuable corporate governance experience in a setting apart from where they spend the bulk of their working time.**

tant than financial compensation. I am sure that some outside directors may be a little offended by this point, but not everyone will be motivated by an offer of more prestige. However, this is certainly a factor for many potential and current directors.

Compensation

For those directors truly worth appointing to the board, the compensation offered will rarely, if ever, represent their true worth to the private companies they serve. Those periodic checks of $50, $100 or even $500 that private companies typically give their directors do not match what these people make doing other things. Stock options are another story and this is where many directors occasionally make some real money. Other compensation methods, perks and benefits are sometimes placed on the table as well. However, no one should base his or her retirement planning on cashing in those founders' shares. That package of financial incentives rarely pays off in real market value relative to the time you put in. Instead, the financials help take the sting out of donating your time and occasionally result in a healthy payoff.

Opportunity to Make a Difference

For the best directors (the kind most boards really want

—and need), this is the most important reason to serve. Many entrepreneurs and other successful people are full of unrealized, or under-realized desires to make the world a better place. Having achieved success themselves, they often look for ways to help others become successful in order to "give something back" to the free enterprise system that allowed them to succeed.

These leaders of our society fill the nonprofit boards of hospitals, churches, boy and girl scouts, and countless other causes. But businesspeople realize that one of the best ways to serve society is to help new and small businesses grow and prosper. They understand that the small business sector of our economy is the most dynamic and most productive in terms of job creation, new product development, productivity improvement and many other key business indicators.

The chance to provide advice and governance to a new company is an exciting opportunity.

The chance to provide advice and governance to a new company is an exciting opportunity that is worth a lot to prospective board members in terms of personal satisfaction. Important and sometimes critical advice is not something just anybody can provide. Being asked to give it can be an irresistible offer to many who are looking for a way to make a real difference in the community, economy and/or society.

Just Because It Is Fun!

Okay, this last one doesn't have quite the starched-shirt, pinstriped ring to it as the other four benefits. Many businesspeople work hard to frown and try to look like business is all work and no play. It sort of makes you feel more important, more serious. But as most really good businessmen and women will tell you, they do business because business is exciting, and well, yes, FUN! Board service is a lot of fun too.

A dynamic, hard working board will let its collective hair down occasionally, either officially at special social functions, or unofficially in the middle of a serious meeting. It may be hard to believe, but boards develop their own cultures, complete with different personality types, usually including a group wise cracker who can bring the house down just when a little release from all that seriousness is most needed—and even when it is not!

Over months and years of working together, boards can develop into tight, effective groups with a high *esprit de corps*. Granted, most of the board time will be hard work, but work itself can be fun, especially when the work is important and successful, and the people like and respect each other.

Summary

These are certainly not the only reasons to serve on private boards, but I believe most people will find this list pretty accurate. If one or more of these benefits appeals to you, then perhaps you should toss your hat into the pool of persons available for board service as a director.

— *Director's Monthly, Vol. 19, No. 5, May 1995*

How To Be An Effective Director

Roger H. Ford, Ph.D.
Zane Showker Professor of Entrepreneurship
James Madison University
Harrisonburg, Virginia

Unfortunately, I know of no school, university or graduate program that teaches about boards of directors. Even in my own M.B.A. course on corporate leadership and strategy, I only devote two weeks to the function of the board. Most directors go into the boardroom a lot like the proverbial child taught how to swim by being tossed into the lake. You

Whether you are an experienced director or the newest one at the table, these tips should serve you well.

"Just do it or drown trying!" Here I will offer a few simple tips on how to be a more effective director. These comments are derived from hundreds of board experiences, observations and interviews with board leaders and directors from hundreds of boards.

1. Know your role.

Being an effective director begins with knowing the role of the board for the business you are serving, and the specific reason you were asked to serve.

Before and Outside of Regular Meetings:
- ✓ **Read** your packet - be prepared!
- ✓ **Seek additional information,** both general and specific to issues.
- ✓ **Seek ways to help and serve your leadership team:**
  - Attend special meetings and retreats.
  - Serve on committees.
  - Attend ceremonies, dinners, etc.
  - Be available as a resource (telephone conferences, lunch meetings, etc.)
- ✓ **Actively fulfill your role** as a board member in the community:
  - Networker
  - Cheerleader
  - Flag-waver
  - *Not* a meddler!

For private companies, the role of the board is frequently more advisory than governance, so it is a good idea to ask the owners or others inviting you to join their board to clarify exactly what they expect from the board. As I have discussed in previous chapters, there are various types of boards, ranging from window dressing to more active boards that actually govern through strategic and/or specific operational duties. You will certainly not be an effective director if you mistakenly see your role as telling the president (who may own 100 percent of the stock) what to do about issues where your opinions were not sought or desired. Start your relationship by responding to what is asked of the board. Other duties and responsibilities may or may not follow.

In nearly every board, the time perspective of relevance is more long term than short term. That is, boards should typically view where the firm is heading in the long term, and what strategies they have to employ to get there.

This long-term attitude is what owners of private companies usually need to hear. They are doing all they can to keep up with the current day-to-day struggles of running the business. Rarely do they need a lot of back-seat driving about daily operations.

In private companies, boards really serve at the pleasure of the owner/entrepreneur. Be sensitive and listen to what is asked of you and try to respond to those specific requests. Leave the back-seat driving to others, at least until you have earned the respect needed to offer unsolicited constructive observations and criticisms.

In private companies, boards really serve at the pleasure of the owner/entrepreneur. Be sensitive and listen to what is asked of you and try to respond to those specific requests.

Directors also need to know their personal role within the board forum. Rarely is a prima donna director effective. A board functions best when its members work together as a team. This suggests that you as an individual director were asked to join the team because of a perception that you had something specific to offer *to that team*.

If your area of expertise is in international marketing, do not be too quick to push your opinions about other ar-

Tips for effective board participation at the meeting
- Listen to others
- Admit your ignorance—ask questions!
- Dig deep—ask *discerning* questions
- Avoid public embarrassment of your leader (ask some questions in private)
- Don't engage in "group think"
- Engage in serious debates—don't be a bystander!
- Don't be petty
- Keep notes where appropriate—they may come in handy later.

eas, such as banking and venture capital, especially if you are not an expert on these issues! Find an appropriate dynamic where you listen to others and contribute according to your abilities and the abilities of others in the group.

As I study board dynamics, I am often reminded of a line in the song, "If I Were A Rich Man," from the musical, "Fiddler on the Roof." In the song, Tevya suggests that if he were rich, his opinion would be sought about everything. The Rabbi would even seek his advice concerning spiritual matters. But Tevya realizes that this would be foolish reasoning because expertise in making money does not make you an expert in all other fields.

So it often is with directors, who sometimes falsely assume that since they are now directors, they must be experts in everything. Not true! A good director will realize that his or her opinion is very useful in some matters, somewhat useful in other issues, and not useful at all in some issues. The important thing is for the board as a whole to realize its role and then for individual directors to participate according to their abilities to serve the group.

2. Allow for an orientation period.

Whether joining a new or established board, some orientation period will be necessary before a new member will feel comfortable, at home and accepted. Some new directors may even experience a period of ritualistic hazing by some of the old-timers! This may consist of nothing more than filling coffee cups, having to endure tired old jokes or war stories or being referred to as "the new kid." Nevertheless, it may be an awkward and uncomfortable time for the newcomer.

Whether joining a new or established board, some orientation period will be necessary before a new member will feel comfortable, at home and accepted.

In this day of hypersensitivity to "political correctness," the initiation period may be even more awkward and uncomfortable. However, these rituals are usually quite harmless, and may even contribute positively to building friendships, trust, respect and *esprit de corps*. In any event, this period will pass soon enough.

The orientation period will go a little more smoothly if the new director takes it all in stride and with good humor. When being asked to get the coffee, remember that it is better to serve than to be served. Almost everyone is impressed when the chairman or CEO takes time to pour coffee or otherwise show respect for the board members. So what is wrong with the newcomer doing likewise? In fact, the new director will earn respect more quickly by showing a little humility towards others who probably have more experience and certainly more seniority.

The new director also needs to avoid coming into a board with a loaded agenda and an attitude that says, "I'm here to serve you and correct all the mistakes you have made." Certainly few directors would say this verbally, but the attitude is sometimes conveyed. Sure, the new director was recruited to bring some new ideas and perspective to the board, but one should never come into a new situation and try to make changes the first day or even in the first few meetings.

3. Be Professional.

A professional attitude and work style will go a long way toward building an effective team. Professionalism means many things. It means being prepared for board meetings, including carefully reviewing your agenda and meeting packet *before* the meeting begins. A director quickly skimming over an agenda and financial statements while the chairman is calling the meeting to order is giving himself or herself away as unprepared. This is rude and other directors who are prepared will not appreciate it, especially if it is a behavior pattern.

Professionalism also means being *on time* for the meetings, and *being prepared to stay until the meeting is adjourned.* Directors who always have to leave early stick out as less committed, so their professional perception suffers. Even if this is the most committed director, it still looks bad!

Professionalism even means getting enough sleep before the meeting so as to be alert and not yawning during someone's comments or presentations. And if you did have to pull a late night, do not brag about it during the board meeting. Everyone else probably works hard too, so they will not be impressed. Why draw attention to the fact that you may be so overextended that your ability to serve the board effectively may be in question?

> **The use of... courtesies such as "please," "thank you," "you're welcome," and "I am sorry," go a long way toward building trust and respect.**

Another point about professionalism is really important to me: that is the importance of having good manners. In this day and age it seems as though everyone has forgotten the simple virtue of politeness. The use of simple courtesies such as, "please," "thank you," "you're welcome"

Boardroom Basics

and "I am sorry," go a long way toward building trust and respect. Likewise, cursing, vulgar jokes, personal attacks, wasting time with irrelevant chatter and negative behaviors of all types will destroy whatever harmony may have existed in a group. Be polite and you are well on your way to being a professional director.

4. Participate.

A director may be the most brilliant and successful member of the community, but if he or she does not participate, that talent is of little use to a board of directors. Good boardroom participants are prepared, they listen to others and they share their views, opinions and experiences. They are sensitive to the opinions of others, yet they avoid "group think" or going along with the crowd just to avoid controversy. And they do these things regularly, and without dominating the meetings.

Directors should periodically review their participation at meetings. Good questions to ask yourself are, "Why did I fail to speak up about the...issue? I had an opinion, but kept my mouth shut. Why?" Or, "Was I dominating that discussion? Was there a reason I was so strongly pushing my ideas? Was I being overly subjective or emotional?" A little honest self-reflection can do wonders to keep individual participation levels at an appropriate level and in balance with other board members.

5. Seek Feedback.

Unfortunately, board memberships do not typically have a formal job description or annual performance appraisal. In fact, the structure of the board for many private companies is so informal that an appointment is often assumed to be a "life term," no questions asked. So how does a director know how he or she is doing? Self-appraisal is certainly useful, but evaluating your own performance is dangerously subjective and inadequate in itself.

Absent from any formal review process, each director should seek outside feedback to ensure that his or her performance is satisfactory, and, hopefully, ever improving.

Absent from any formal review process, each director should seek outside feedback to ensure that his or her performance is satisfactory, and, hopefully, ever improving.

A good starting place is to simply ask the chairman or CEO to honestly tell you what they think about your effectiveness as a director. Try to avoid catching them off guard or putting them on the spot. Perhaps suggest a lunch or breakfast meeting, and let them know in advance what you want to talk about so your evaluator has a chance to think about it. Accept whatever they tell you politely, even if you do not like what you hear. You may even suggest the board develop a formal process of board and board member review and appraisal.

Another good source of feedback can come from fellow directors. Even if the company president tells you that he thinks you walk on water, your peers will view you differently from company leadership, so their perspectives should occasionally be sought. Simply tell another director that you are doing a self-evaluation and want some feedback on how he or she thinks you are performing as a director. You will probably be pleasantly surprised how positively this sort of question is received. Nearly everyone respects someone who is earnestly trying to do a better job.

Of course, do not overdo it. You do not need to seek input from every director, nor do you need to ask for this kind of feedback often. But if you have served on a board for a year or two and have never received any kind of feedback, now may be the time.

6. If you are not contributing, resign!

Getting asked to serve on a board is a nice experience. You feel positive about yourself because someone else expresses confidence in your ability to contribute at such a high level of responsibility. However, sometimes the director-elect can confuse flattery with fit. Just because you have an invitation, does not necessarily mean it is right for you.

Occasionally, I receive calls and letters from company presidents who want my advice on how to get onto some other boards. This leads me to suspect that rarely will a board candidate ask the question, "Can I *contribute* to this company?" Yet many boards have at least one board member who really should not serve—not necessarily because the director is incompetent, but because it is just not a good fit.

7. Final Advice

My final advice concerning effectiveness is this: Do not accept an invitation to serve unless you really think you can contribute and you intend to work hard to do so. And, if after some interval of board service you feel you are not contributing, resign and get out of the way! You will be less frustrated finding a better place to serve and the board will be healthier too. I do not really think there are all that many board members who are *incapable* of being good directors, but there certainly are many who simply do not make the effort or do not have the knowledge and training to be effective.

— *Director's Monthly, Vol. 19, No. 7, July 1995*

Chapter Four:
THE BOARD IN ACTION
Success And Failure In The Boardroom Battlefield

I am deeply indebted to two guest authors and a co-author for the articles contained in this chapter. To give readers deeper insights as to the detailed workings of boards in action, I turned to respected experts for assistance. The first article was written with my colleague, Dr. Marion White, an international management expert and professor. Her interest in the failed takeover attempt of WLR Foods by poultry giant Tyson Foods was based in part on the question of how the cultures of two very different firms might clash or gel, depending on the takeover outcome.

The other articles are both solo efforts by respected professionals. First, Dr. Warren Braun describes how his board of directors helped transform his engineering/manufacturing enterprise from a 100 percent entrepreneur-owned firm to a 100 percent employee-owned firm. Next, Dr. Stanley Vance discusses how another entrepreneurial-run firm failed to utilize its board to maximum performance, resulting in a less-than-ideal outcome.

Battle of the Boards:
Tyson vs. WLR Foods

Marion M. White, Ph.D.
Associate Professor of Management

Roger H. Ford, Ph.D.
Zane Showker Professor of Entrepreneurship
James Madison University
Harrisonburg, Virginia

"A Question of Timing" in chapter two pointed out that the best time to build a strong and effective board is before you need it. It offered as an example the well-established board at Virginia-based WLR Foods, Inc., a fully integrated producer of turkey and chicken products, and the pivotal role that it played in fending off the hostile takeover attempt by Arkansas raider Don Tyson of Tyson Foods.

At the beginning of 1994, WLR Foods, Inc., looked like an easy takeover target for Tyson.

This was the first major defeat for Tyson. Previously Tyson had grown to be the country's largest poultry producer by acquiring more than a dozen of its competitors. In 1994, with sales of approximately $5 billion, Tyson was five times larger than WLR.

This "David and Goliath" tale raises several important questions: How and why did WLR succeed? What role did the board and individual directors play? What are the implications of this battle?

Some readers may wonder why we would use a case from a public company like WLR to illustrate issues related to private boards. While it is true that WLR is publicly traded and has several thousand shareholders, it still exhibits many characteristics of private and family-owned companies. In fact, not too many years ago, WLR was comprised of several smaller, family-owned companies that merged to create a market for their companies' stock. Many of the original entrepreneurs and family member owner/managers are still on the scene today as shareholders, officers and directors of the WLR organization. When the situation became serious during the summer takeover initiative, the leadership group was able to command an impressive majority control, in spite of the fact that an attractive financial offer was on the table. While it may be true that money talks, this case proves that it doesn't always deliver. Therefore, we feel that the lessons here are useful for directors of private as well as public firms.

Sequence of Events

At the beginning of 1994, WLR Foods, Inc., looked like an easy takeover target for Tyson. WLR had just completed a five-year, $150 million expansion that had depressed the company's stock price. Tyson offered to buy the company for $30 a share, representing a 57 percent premium over the $19 closing price for WLR stock on the day the offer was announced. Wall Street analysts predicted that this was a done deal.

WLR Defensive Maneuvers

During the next few months, the WLR board took several actions that helped the company fend off Tyson:

- On January 24, after Tyson made its takeover bid public, WLR stock rose to about $29 a share in anticipation of quick profits by arbitrageurs.

WLR management and key directors simply did not want to lose control of their company regardless of the financial ramifications of the proposed deal.

- On February 6, the WLR board unanimously rejected Tyson's $329 million or $30 a share offer as being inadequate. The official reason stated was that the Tyson offer did not reflect the true expected value of the company. However, others have speculated that WLR management and key directors simply did not want to lose control of their company, regardless of the financial ramifications of the proposed deal.

- At the same time, the board adopted a "Shareholder Protection Rights Plan" that would effectively dilute the holdings of anyone acquiring 15 percent or more of WLR stock. Under this plan, in the event of a takeover attempt, shareholders have the right to acquire one additional share at half price for each rights certificate held. Tyson immediately challenged the legality of this shareholder protection plan and filed a lawsuit. Many observers applauded this aggressive response by the WLR board to protect its independence from Tyson.

- In another maneuver on February 6, four members of WLR's board of directors resigned from their paid positions with the company so they could legally vote as shareholders on the controversial issues involving the takeover effort. Unless successfully challenged in court by Tyson, this move assured that the 13.8 percent of shares held by these four directors would not have to sit out the game's crucial future plays.

- On March 9, Tyson announced its tender offer at $30 a share. By April 7, Tyson had received only seven percent of WLR shares. On May 21, at a special shareholders meeting, over 70 percent of WLR shareholders voted not to allow Tyson to have voting rights attached to their shares, as recommended by the WLR board.

- On June 3 and again on July 29, Tyson extended its offer. It now had 21 percent of common stock tendered. In another surprise development on July 28, WLR's board moved to acquire North Carolina turkey company, Cuddy Farms, Inc., for $73.8 million, paid with $43 million in cash and WLR stock. This pre-emptive deal put an additional 10 percent of WLR stock in "friendly" hands, and may have effectively killed the deal for Tyson.

• Finally, on August 4, Tyson announced its decision to terminate its offer. It was expected that they would again extend the deadline; however, Tyson threw in the towel realizing it could not gather the votes needed for victory. That night, WLR stock closed at $22.25, signaling Wall Street's decision that the $30 offer was dead. By early 1995, WLR was again trading in the $26 per share range.

> **The single most important factor for WLR in rebuffing Tyson was the presence of a strong board willing to stand up for what it believed in.**

Keys to Victory

In the October 1994 issue of *Turkey World*, WLR Foods CEO James Keeler commented that the single most important factor in WLR rebuffing Tyson was the presence of a strong board willing to stand up for what it believed in. When the board recommended rejecting the $30 per share offer, more than 70 percent of the shareholders agreed. How did the WLR board manage to command such loyalty, especially in the face of a quick 57 percent profit?

There is no doubt that the board was well established

and trusted. The two key directors are Charles Wampler, Jr., a member of the board since 1976 and board chairman since 1984, and WLR President and CEO James Keeler, a director since 1988. This board's ties to the poultry industry run deep. For example, Charles Wampler, Sr., founded the Wampler Company with his two brothers in 1927.

According to one management-level employee, Charles Wampler, Jr., played the greatest role, closely followed by Keeler, who played a less visible role but was responsible for the complex legal and financial maneuvers the company undertook during the takeover attempt.

Wampler enjoys a reputation of being very active in the local community. For example, he helped found the local United Way and was its first chairman. The other 10 board members are also widely respected in the community.

Community leaders expressed support for WLR's effort to remain independent, as did numerous letters in the local press from shareholders, employees and growers. WLR is referred to as "family" in the Shenandoah Valley. The company takes pride in its management living in and being part of the local community. WLR has about 600 employees and 400 growers in Virginia, and, according to one employee, a large percentage of its stock is held within 100 miles of WLR's home office. Therefore, it should come as no surprise that public opinion in the area strongly supported WLR's position.

In contrast, Don Tyson was often portrayed as a villain during the ordeal. Despite advertisements placed in the local press and several trips by Tyson to the area to talk to WLR growers (many of whom are shareholders), most were never convinced that Tyson would keep his promises. In fact, the aforementioned WLR employee stated that many had the feeling Tyson and his "puppet board" were willing to say or do anything to get WLR stockholders to sell. Therefore, Tyson was not trusted.

Timing may also have been a factor. Throughout the Tyson/WLR battle, Tyson was frequently mentioned in other less-than-favorable media stories due to his affiliation with Hillary Clinton, a former Tyson board member. None of this aided Tyson's popularity in heavily conservative rural Virginia.

> **Tyson was often portrayed as a villain during the ordeal... most were never convinced that Tyson would keep his promises.**

Implications

There can be no doubt that WLR's strong board played a crucial role in fending off the Tyson takeover attempt. At the same time, it must be remembered that this company spent decades building excellent relationships with shareholders, employees, growers, buyers and the community at large. Collectively, this forms the company's base, and this is from where the crucial support for WLR came.

— *Director's Monthly, Vol. 19, No. 1, January 1995*

Relinquishing the Helm

Warren L. Braun, P.E.
Chairman of the Board, ComSonics, Inc.
Harrisonburg, Virginia

Is there life after the presidency? Do you miss the perks of the executive washroom? Do you regret leaving the post of ultimate power? All these questions and many more were ones I had to ask myself prior to stepping aside as president, CEO and chairman of ComSonics, a company I started in 1972.

A visionary CEO, a strong board and dedicated employees made this a success story.

Now, for a bit of background. ComSonics was formed as a technical service enterprise serving the cable television industry. Along the way, its management team developed unique and proprietary products that enhanced the market development of the company. The firm has become a worldwide organization, marketing both directly and through agents in 15 countries, mostly in the Pacific Rim. From a company with 22 employees, mostly part-time, it has grown to 156 full-time employees.

Decision

As the founder and original sole owner of the corporation, I had made the decision to ultimately turn the ownership of the company over to the employees. After examining a variety of concepts, I decided in 1974 to form the corporation as an employee stock ownership plan (ESOP) with 100 percent of the ownership to be transferred to the employees upon my retirement. The step by step process by which this was accomplished in 1975 is detailed in my book, *"On the Way to Successful Employee Ownership."*

The transition from 100 percent ownership by me to total ownership by the employees was one I had thought over many times during my years of ownership. I carefully measured the performance of each of the executives reporting to me for their leadership capability. I did not see a "successor in my image," but I *did* determine that one employee had the necessary ability and personality to become the next president, although I was sure his management style would be quite different from mine. Confident in that employee's abilities and in the employee group as a whole, I transferred my last block of stock into the ESOP in 1985 with a leveraged buy-out, making a personal guarantee for the loan. To back this financial commitment, which caused me some concern, I decided I would continue as president, CEO and chairman until the loan guarantee was removed some five years later in 1990.

Changing of the Guards

In 1990, with some considerable fanfare, the new president and CEO was installed and I remained as chairman. I made it very clear to him that the "ball was in his court," and I was not about to be "up-to-plate" anymore. I reduced my public appearances as a corporate officer to the absolute minimum to give him ample room to grow in the community and generally, I stayed out of his hair. During this time, I met with our new president once a week to discuss any non-operational issues that I felt were important. I also chaired the quarterly board meetings.

When I structured the corporation as an ESOP, I thought it advisable to set up the board of directors in such a way as to enhance the role of governance of the board—*not* to serve as an alter ego for the president—to broaden the perspective of each of the employee stockholders.

When I structured the corporation as an ESOP, I thought it advisable to set up the board of directors in such a way as to enhance the role of governance of the board—not to serve as an alter ego for the president.

The board was structured with membership from within the corporation balanced by equal membership from outside individuals solicited for their business acumen and knowledge of our field.

The present external board membership is comprised

of an ESOP specialist, a CPA with strong financial ties including ownership in the cable television industry, a retired corporate vice president from a *Fortune* 100 company with specialized expertise in executive training, and a local businessman/attorney with extensive knowledge of business development. The final external board member has served as a human relations consultant to the corporation for several years.

An equal number of board members are elected "at large" from the employee stockholders' base, with the chairman of the employee advisory committee being an automatic board member.

Does such a combination of board members work? I believe this board composition is *very* satisfactory. They meet every three months in what I would call a "creative dissent" environment.

But what about me? Do I miss being president? Quite frankly, no. I believe not, partly because I had made the decision to make this transition and partly because I found our new president to be both capable and competent. He took my advice to visit all our top customers personally and he did a splendid job of hastening the transition to his presence as president/CEO.

Does this mean that the transition was all sweetness and light? Of course not. There were a few moments of tension when some of the board members criticized our new president for his performance during the transition period. I am sure he found this uncomfortable, but it was part of his training in becoming president.

Temptation

Unfortunately, the year he ascended to the office of president, the market for our products turned sour and the corporation lost a considerable amount of money. I was tempted to pick up the reins, but I knew that he would never learn how to crisis manage unless he saw this through on his own.

My confidence proved to be well placed. He became a successful president/CEO.

> **My role continues as an adviser and, I hope, as a good listener. I offer very little advice unless asked.**

He turned the corporation around and had a very acceptable performance with the corporation sailing into a meteoric year in fiscal 1993-1994. I am glad I didn't intervene. His solutions to problems were not of the usual downsizing variety so typical of many managers today. Instead, he elected to accelerate new product development and he pushed hard for more aggressive sales/marketing. He is well on the way to becoming a very savvy CEO.

My role continues as an adviser and, I hope, as a good listener. I offer very little advice unless asked. I rarely go to my office at the plant (which is much smaller than the one I occupied as president) more than two or three hours per week. I have relegated my role to that of being a seer, i.e., an analyst for the future of "their" business, as I no longer own any stock in the firm. Hopefully, what I do is of value. From the collective comments coming from the board and the president, at least for the present, that is true.

Life after ComSonics

Well, what do I do with all the time left over? First off, I was never a workaholic. I believed that a long work week does not necessarily indicate excellent management. I have always had a strong ambition to write, which I fulfilled to a modest degree upon relinquishing the presidency. My books are: *"On the Way to Successful Employee Ownership,"* and *"Dear God: Why Am I Here?"* The books have no connection, they are simply where my mind wanted to take me at the time. I am currently writing a novel, *"A Glimpse Behind the Veil."* I have also completed a Christmas play entitled, *"A Gift of Love."* I have a set of well-developed hobbies: woodworking and gardening. Both were long-held hobby pursuits of mine and I enjoy them a lot, although I don't spend a great deal more time with them than I did before I retired.

Currently, I serve on several boards: our local educational television station, the executive advisory committee of the School of Business at James Madison University and the board of trustees at Shenandoah University.

As many have said of retirement, "I don't know how I will meet all the time pressures I have *now.*" Fortunately, most of these pressures are ones I can change and I am careful not to accumulate new demands on my time. Am I glad to be retired from the position of president? You bet! I am especially pleased to see the employee owners doing such a fine job managing, growing and nurturing "their" company. I am very pleased to see that the faith I had in them was well placed.

— *Director's Monthly, Vol. 18, No. 7, July 1994*

"All The Tire Tracks Stopped Here"
A Leader's Lesson

Stanley C. Vance, Ph.D.
William B. Stokely Professor Emeritus
Department of Management
University of Tennessee
Knoxville, Tennessee

"The bigger, the better." That is how most of us consider scale of enterprise. Wrong. If this were a fact, then virtually all of the millions of small-scale companies, including start-ups, family firms, closely held ventures and the like, would get very low scores on our quality scale. But, as every Izaak Waltonian knows, tiny minnows have distinct advantages—they are agile and they can get into tiny crevices for food and shelter. Unfortunately, they cannot always outswim their bigger brethren. This fact, rather than any lack of quality, explains the unfortunate demise of the medium-sized Seiberling Rubber Company, which, after years of successful maneuvering, eventually was gobbled up.

> **The best of companies ...need more than one leader to survive the rough roads of corporate change.**

Akron

Back in the mid- to late-1950s, before the ill-fated showdown between the Ohio National Guard and student demonstrators took place, I was dean of Kent State's 2000-student College of Business Administration. There I had the marvelous opportunity to get acquainted with the Akron-area business community. Among its leaders were top executives of most of the nation's leading rubber companies, including Goodyear, Goodrich, Firestone, General Tire and Seiberling. This was a tremendous break for me. Earlier in my career, I had set my sights on corporate governance and I had been waiting for a chance to focus on some real boardrooms. I had a splendid opportunity to do just that in Akron.

My proximity to an entire industry's leadership put me on the cutting edge of scholarship. I even ventured to build an imposing statistical model using regression analysis to compare company structure and performance. More importantly, I was provided intimate case studies involving real corporate decision-makers.

Scion

One such mover and shaker was J. Penfield Seiberling, scion and CEO of one of the rubber industry's founding families. His firm had helped make Akron the capital of the world's rubber industry. In my first interview with Seiberling in 1961 conducted in his Akron company headquarters, I learned there was to be a significant transformation. The Seiberling firm was about to lose its autonomy and identity to one of the new breed of corporate "raiders." While the classic raiders are long gone, their marauding lingers on in takeovers with euphemistic labels such as acquisition, buy-out and, most saccharine of all, merger. Raiding, by whatever name, is a serious threat to all publicly held companies, particularly smaller ones.

The raider in this instance was fellow Ohioan Edward O. Lamb, operating out of Toledo. Lamb initiated his Seiberling takeover campaign in 1955 and succeeded in getting control in 1962. His takeover formula was very simple. Find a small-scale, successful enterprise in a growing industry where the intended victim is under-capitalized, with a book value far greater than its market valuation. Seiberling easily met this prescription. There were only 587,000 shares outstanding—a raider's dream. Coupled with this was the relatively low $9 per share price and the higher net asset value of $23 per share. Evidently, the firm was worth more dead than alive. Lamb paid about $5 million to gain ownership control.

Raiding, by whatever name, is a serious threat to all publicly held companies.

In three of the next four years, as raiding turned to gutting via divestitures, Lamb's Seiberling acquisition lost money. But eventually, Lamb sold off the rubber processing facilities for $31 million, a fantastic payoff for terminating the life of a rubber industry pioneer.

End of the Line

How could the company's owners have failed to know and communicate the company's real worth? I dared to ask Seiberling why the top corporate heads had not counseled him to fight the raid. Where was his president, chief operating officer, chief financial officer and other concerned and informed competent members of his team? He then explained that his company had no such ranking executives with meaningful power. Seiberling not only represented the family as major stockholder, he was also the president, CEO, COO, CFO, CAO and all other pertinent alphabetical designations. He readily admitted that he should have expanded the company's control mechanism to include other dedicated and knowledgeable members of his staff. Unfortunately, he was the final authority. As he put it, "All the tire tracks stopped here."

This founder's reluctance to share titles and authority seems to be congenital to most small-scale family firms, even publicly held firms. Too often, recognition of this de-

"All The Tire Tracks Stopped Here"

fect comes too late. After years of successfully "operating by the seat of the pants," suddenly the decision-maker finds he has outgrown his corporate britches.

Not Unique

But this concentration of leadership is not unique to family-owned firms. A third of a century after my enlightening conversation with Seiberling, the center of corporate gravity in larger companies is shifting inward.

In the past, larger companies tended to differentiate between the two polar power centers—the chairman and the president. Currently, these two roles have been combined in at least one-third of our larger corporations as follows: Chairman/CEO 50%; *Chairman/CEO/President 35%;* President/CEO 15%.

> **In the past, larger companies tended to differentiate between the two polar power centers—the chairman and the president. Currently, these two roles have been combined in at least one-third of our larger corporations.**

This data comes from a summary of *Business Week's* "Executive Compensation Scoreboard," April 25, 1994, which covers almost 500 executives in 36 industry categories. Interestingly, the Rubber Tire Group includes only two companies, Goodyear and Cooper, with several of the former leaders now casualties of takeovers. The tire industry certainly has shriveled from the score plus companies

Boardroom Basics

of a generation ago. A percentage of this slump may be attributed to the shift in boardroom governance toward combining the chairmanship and the presidency in some of the nation's largest firms.

These large firms have tried to spread control with the Office of the President, co-chairmen/presidents, worker ownership via employee stock ownership plans, the more ambitious UAL venture and in Germany, *Mitbestimmungsrecht,* but no experiment seems to have taken hold. Big companies have returned to undisputed rule by the all-encompassing chairman of the board. Although the locus of control has shifted from president to chairman, the effect is the same.

Today, both large and small companies are showing a preference for Seiberling's one-man rule, even in the rubber industry, where new players Bridgestone, Michelin, and Continental have taken over from the old guard. None of them seem to have learned from Seiberling's rueful admission that, "All the tire tracks stopped here."

— *Director's Monthly, Vol. 18, No. 9, September 1994*

Chapter Five:
SPECIAL CASES -
Start-Up, Family And International Boards

Over the years, I have frequently cautioned that boards of directors are not for everybody or for every firm. In fact, I have often been concerned that private company owners sometimes turn to the board for the wrong reasons and with unreasonable expectations. They may naively see the board as some sort of a savior or panacea for whatever and all problems their firm may be facing. However, my primary conviction is that the board can be an excellent tool for most any company. But there are some situations where the board may not be as useful or not as easy to establish. Three of these situations are: 1) during start-up for a new firm, 2) for the family-run firm and 3) in international situations where the cross-cultural, political and economic complications are particularly acute. The articles in this chapter address each of these situations.

The first article, co-authored with Dr. S. Michael Camp, discusses the role of the board for start-up companies. Entrepreneurs and their boards often see the world quite differently—the entrepreneur being aggressive and optimis-

tic, while the board is cautious and reserved. How to reconcile these competing perspectives is a difficult issue. The next article, co-authored with Dr. Karen W. Wigginton, explores the role of the board in family-run firms. The board can bring many strengths to family businesses, which often run into problems of nepotism and subjectivity, especially as the firm and family member involvement grows over time. Finally, I offer two articles about my experiences in trying to help establish a board of directors for a new coconut venture in the Socialist Republic of Vietnam.

The Role Of The Board During Start-up

S. Michael Camp, Ph.D.
Director, National Center for Entrepreneurial Research,
The Kauffman Foundation
Kansas City, Missouri

Roger H. Ford, Ph.D.
Zane Showker Professor of Entrepreneurship
James Madison University
Harrisonburg, Virginia

How establishing a board early in a new venture can benefit start-up.

Businesses, like people, experience a variety of special situations as they grow and mature. One of the most unique periods in the life of a business is its start-up—the time period from its conceptualization as a venture to its stabilization as an operating business.

Though the characteristics of start-up are relatively common across different types of ventures, start-up duration can range from one to five years or even longer, depending on the experience of the entrepreneurial team and the complexity of the new opportunity. Experts report that the failure rate for start-ups is approximately 25 percent within the first two years and as much as 50 percent in the first five years. The risk may be even higher when considering that many potential new ventures never make it out of the dream stage. These ventures could be viewed as having failed before they really began.

During start-up, critical decisions must be made about how to structure, position and finance the venture—all against a backdrop of uncertainty. This includes uncertainty about critical matters such as the size and growth of the market, the reaction of entrenched competition, the demand for the new product or service, the availability of key resources, the feasibility of innovative technologies and the timing of the window of opportunity. To successfully manage in situations of such great uncertainty, the entrepreneur needs to either possess extraordinary knowledge, talent and skills, or count on others who possess the necessary skills. In addition to the expertise of key managers and outsiders, an active board of directors can help the entrepreneur successfully navigate the start-up process.

"Start-up" Defined

The start-up process consists of three distinct phases: pre-entry, market entry and early growth. Each of these stages has unique challenges for the entrepreneur and unique questions for the board of directors. The distinguishing features of each phase and how an active board can benefit the venture along the way are briefly described as follows:

Pre-Entry (1-12 months)

Pre-entry, sometimes called the embryonic or seed stage, is when dreams and ideas are turned into plans for market entry. The substance of each plan depends to a large degree on the intentions of the lead entrepreneur. During this phase, the initial emphasis is on feasibility study, prototype development and/or market testing. Once the entrepreneur has determined that the business idea is feasible, the task shifts to designing an organization and procuring the resources needed to pursue specific objectives. Most of the entrepreneur's energy is spent scanning the environment, developing the appropriate entry strategy, marshaling resources and completing any details in the final product/service offering.

> **Once the entrepreneur has determined that the business idea is feasible, the task shifts to designing an organization and procuring the resources needed.**

Many entrepreneurs are capable of handling this early phase completely solo. However, for more complicated venture ideas, or where the entrepreneur has less experience, the early development of a board brings many advantages to the project. We know of many such firms where the board was recruited even before the incorporation papers were filed or the firm even had a name.

Successful ventures ranging from banks, private

schools, medical practices, to electronic manufacturers and countless others were all started with board members contributing to the creative and research processes. Most of these ventures are led by a strong, capable entrepreneur, yet they all bear the marks of the entire venture team. Many aspects of the pre-entry situation are uncertain, including the size and nature of the market, the strategy and position of leading competitors, the role of the management team, the cost of materials, equipment, facilities and capital and the most effective market entry strategy. This strategy should be based on relevant industry experience. If the entrepreneur lacks this experience, he or she should seek it from others—ideally from a board of directors.

Market Entry (6-18 months)

Market entry begins with the first customer order or sale and continues until manufacturing, distribution and sales operations are firmly established. As the entrepreneur drives this phase of the process, much of the day-to-day implementation of the entry plan may be delegated to the management team or even to board members.

For a number of reasons, board members often report taking a very active role during market entry. First, assuming that the board played a role in developing the conceptual foundation for the venture, it is only natural that they would also take a "hands-on" role in the actual early implementation of the business.

Second, sometimes board members "help out" with implementation simply because there is no one else to help the lead entrepreneur and he or she clearly needs help. During start-up, board members often sell stock through their personal networks, raise capital through venture capitalists or banks, recruit key employees and help locate property or plant space. They can also work at more creative functions like development of advertising and marketing plans. We know board members who came up with the company name and logo, wrote print ads, developed personnel and policy manuals and even moved furniture!

Finally, board members often are active during start-up because they enjoy it. The start-up activity of any new venture can be very exciting, and board members may pour a large amount of their personal (and usually unpaid) energy into the process.

> **Sometimes board members "help out" with implementation simply because there is no one else to help the lead entrepreneur and he or she clearly needs help.**

The key tasks of market entry involve very specific short-term goals such as securing properties and lease arrangements, constructing facilities, closing on capital programs for source of funds, securing the early management team and serving initial customers. It is also at this point that the lead entrepreneur begins to test his or her initial beliefs about the future of the business and whether the idea has the same value (profit potential) as originally thought. It is common for entrepreneurs to view their world and their work through rose-colored glasses. They may need the perspective of board members to honestly assess their initial performance and market success. Directors can be far more objective than the lead entrepreneur.

Early Growth (24-48 months)

The focus of the early growth phase is on stabilizing the operations or reaching a point of legitimacy for the new venture. Stabilizing operations is the most time-consuming start-up task and it can be the most complex for the lead entrepreneur. This period is characterized by a moderate level of uncertainty given management's preparation for accelerated growth. Various financial and operational control systems are being designed as a result of successful market entry and a greater understanding of how to effectively compete in the chosen market.

The role of the lead entrepreneur at this point is twofold—bringing stability to the growing operations and setting the future growth agenda. His or her role moves beyond that of a visionary and shifts to that of a true leader. It is exactly this role transition and the entrepreneur's changing responsibilities that make this phase of start-up difficult for all involved. Which areas of responsibility need their close control and which can be effectively delegated?

Though the process can be difficult, most entrepreneurs understand that the single greatest threat to the future growth of the business is their inability or unwillingness to delegate as their role changes. The board can play a key role here as a bridge from the pioneering start-up organization, to the more professional organization needed to lead the firm into the future. The board members can provide stability, continuity and valuable connections into the growing web of relationships the new firm is experiencing.

> **The board can play a key role as a bridge from the pioneering start-up organization to the more professional organization needed to lead the firm into the future.**

The Advantages Of An "Active" Board of Directors

How active should the board be in the decision-making process? Two factors ultimately determine the answer:

- the degree to which the entrepreneur possesses the skills and experience required to successfully manage the venture, and
- how much control he or she is willing to relinquish over the decision-making process.

There are several ways boards have been shown to benefit their businesses. The most common ways an active board can benefit a start-up venture include networking, formulating business strategy, establishing governance policy, conducting independent assessments, providing specialized expertise, managing in crisis situations and overseeing change and innovation.

However, regardless of when the board is introduced there are a few basic considerations when using a board during the start-up process. The key to establishing an effective board for the start-up of a new venture is to look for experience that the entrepreneurial team lacks. More often than not, this means going outside the firm for specialized expertise. The advantages to having outside directors include:

- added credibility for the firm
- assistance with making major management decisions
- access to additional management expertise not otherwise available
- an unbiased outlook on the future of the company
- a fresh perspective on many issues.

Studies have linked the presence of outside directors with superior performance among young entrepreneurial ventures.

The initial board should consist of no more than five directors, with at least three from outside the organization. (It is easier to add more directors later than to get rid of them after recruiting too many!) The chosen outside directors should be experienced in as many aspects of the new venture as possible, including the start-up process, the industry, the product technology and the specific target market.

When recruiting directors, be realistic about the skills required and the level of commitment expected. Prospects should know the specific issues for which their expertise is being sought so they can make an informed decision before joining.

Involving a board of directors during start-up may seem counterintuitive to the typical entrepreneur, who views himself or herself as a rugged individual preparing to go it alone against the world. While many such maverick type entrepreneurs do succeed, many will find greater success much faster and with fewer breakdowns along the way by taking along a few strong directors to help negotiate the trail.

The outside directors should be experienced in as many aspects of the new venture as possible.

— *Director's Monthly, Vol. 21, No. 3, March 1997*

Boards Of Directors And The Family-Owned Business

Roger H. Ford, Ph.D.
Zane Showker Professor of Entrepreneurship

Karen W. Wigginton, Ed.D.
Director, Small Business Development Center
James Madison University
Harrisonburg, Virginia

Family-owned businesses face challenges which are often unfamiliar to non-family businesses. For this article, we define a family-owned business as one in which two or more family members own and operate the business. Family firms must deal with many special problems which other private firms may not face. For example, family business owners often make decisions where family and business issues overlap. They may also struggle to name a successor due to sibling rivalry. The number of family-owned businesses moving on to the next generation are decreasing, while the complex problems they encounter continue to impose on the future of the business. The family business owner is constantly

> **The number of family-owned businesses moving on to the next generation are decreasing while the complex problems they encounter continue to impose on the future of the business.**

caught between doing what is best for the business and keeping peace in the family. Unfortunately, long-range strategic planning for the business is often avoided due to the complexities involved in decision-making and the problems that may arise as a result of these decisions. When crises come, it may be too late to respond effectively.

In these and other instances, boards of directors can be beneficial to both the family and the business. While all problems cannot be solved through a board, outside boards of directors can help families better manage their businesses. They can provide specialized areas of expertise with an objective viewpoint that considers the best interests of the business and the family. They can even arbitrate among feuding family members. The primary purpose of the board for the family-run enterprise is to provide overall management assistance to the business owners and to contribute to the continuity, growth and welfare of the business. Although a board of directors may not be necessary for every family-run business, it can prove to be the guiding factor that leads some family-owned businesses successfully into future generations.

Inside Board vs. Outside Board

Creating an effective board of directors takes a lot of time and effort, but can prove to be beneficial for a family business if the owner commits to the process of recruiting, educating and training the directors, as well as continually assessing the contributions of the board members. Family-owned businesses choosing to form a board of directors must decide on the composition of that board. The board may be composed of insiders, outsiders or preferably a combination of both. Each business owner must assess the needs of the business and tailor the board to meet those needs.

Proponents of outside boards in the family-owned business suggest that these directors provide greater influence and assistance than insider-dominated boards because of their objectivity and expertise. Some have suggested that insider-dominated boards may often act in their own self-interest and not in the best interests of the business. While there is some research that supports this viewpoint, there are other studies that support the value of inside boards of directors. Pioneer studies by Stanley Vance and later research by co-author Roger Ford indicate that the value of insider-dominated boards is their knowledge of the business, its technology and processes, commitment to the business, and availability. Some business owners simply avoid outside directors because they believe they will be giving up control of the business. However, proponents of outside directors suggest that outsiders on the family business boards provide objective guidance for the future success of the owner and the business. Regardless of the composition of a board, co-author Ford believes that, "Insiders need to learn how to become generalists, rather than specialists. Outsiders need to become familiar with the basic affairs, products, people, and philosophy of the firm." Together, the combined membership of the board can become a powerful asset to the family-owned firm.

Benefits of a Board of Directors

There are several areas where a board of directors can provide great benefit to a family-run business. First, boards of directors can assist family business owners with succession planning. Succession planning can be a difficult process for many family-owned businesses to the point that some owners elect not to engage in the process. In other words, succession may be dictated by an executor of the family or even the courts following the death of a company's founder. A board of directors can provide direction and assistance through a carefully managed succession process. A board can assist with everything from planning the process and screening candidates to selecting, preparing, training and evaluating the successor. Having the board assist with these decisions offers an objective viewpoint geared toward doing what is best for the family and the future success of the business. It can also place less pressure on the family business owner when other family members understand that decisions related to succession are made with input from other successful business owners or key advisors such as bankers and attorneys. Additionally, some family business owners are hesitant to turn the business over to a successor because it means that they relinquish control of the business. A board can assist the family business owner in preparing well in advance for succession so that passing on the business to the next generation is a smooth transition for the successor and the family business owner.

A board can assist the family business owner in preparing well in advance for succession so that passing on the business to the next generation is a smooth transition.

Second, no family or business exists without problems or issues that arise from time to time. A family business owner can often get caught up in the overlap between family and business when trying to make decisions related to both. He or she wants to make good business decisions while maintaining peace in the family. A board of directors can assist with family and business issues by providing objective insight into decisions that affect the family and the business. For example, we have noticed that it sometimes takes an outsider to convince a leader to take that long overdue family vacation. The strong-willed entrepreneur is less likely to listen to his or her family about such things!

Third, directors can assist family-owned businesses with strategic planning for the family and the business. While the development of a business plan is the responsibility of top management, directors can provide assistance by reviewing the plan and raising questions that may need to be addressed. A common reason why businesses create a board of directors is for assistance in strategic and long-range planning. This insight is valuable because of the expertise and experiences that the directors bring to the table. Likewise, the board can provide counsel or raise questions related to strategic planning for the family in matters such as succession and estate planning. Related to the future success of the business is the future of the family members. Since the primary asset of the *family* is the *business*, it is inevitable that the family and business alike must be considered in any meaningful planning process. The board can assist these individuals in developing a plan of action for themselves as it relates to their future goals and position in the family business. The board's guidance can help formulate the future roles and responsibilities of these individuals in the family business.

— *Director's Monthly, Vol. 21, No. 7, July 1997*

Dispatch From Hanoi:
Creating A Board Of Directors In The Socialist Republic Of Vietnam

Roger H. Ford, Ph.D.
Zane Showker Professor of Entrepreneurship
James Madison University
Harrisonburg, Virginia

In 1996, I had the unique experience of helping create a small desiccated coconut enterprise in Ben Tre, Vietnam, a rural province located on an island south of Saigon. This enterprise was to have a Western-style board of directors, which is the focus of this article. But first, a little background is needed.

Exporting U.S.-style corporate governance requires good faith, patience and a spirit of partnership.

In 1993, IDEVN, a North American nonprofit organization, was asked to help develop a coconut project begun by the Swedish Red Cross in Hue, a province in central Vietnam. The Swedish Red Cross had invested a lot of time, energy and money in an attempt to help Vietnam enter the desiccated coconut industry, which is the manufacture of dried coconut used in the candy and cookie industries. Vietnam's only previous attempt at entering this industry niche failed miserably after an early export shipment of finished product was found to be contaminated.

IDEVN is part of IDE International, an American/Canadian non-governmental, nonprofit organization (NGO), engaged in helping the world's poor by providing affordable, appropriate technologies to rural farmers. In Vietnam, IDE's primary focus was on manual irrigation via the manufacture and marketing of a variety of treadle (foot power) and hand pumps. What makes IDE's approach unique is that, unlike its giant cousin UNICEF, IDE believes the world's poor should be treated as customers who are willing to pay for their goods and services, as long as the price and quality is right. Therefore, IDE's activities revolve around developing less expensive pumps and distribution methods and working with Vietnam's own emerging industrial and entrepreneurial class. Hence, the IDE pump line is considerably cheaper than those offered by UNICEF, a fact that is well known to UNICEF. The two organizations were negotiating ways to work more closely together.

IDEVN's reputation for entrepreneurial approaches and know-how contributed to the Swedish Red Cross's request to help salvage the struggling coconut project. In January 1994, IDE brought young English engineer Dan Salter to Vietnam to head up the coconut project. His job was to determine if it was technically and economically feasible to produce desiccated coconut in Vietnam.

Salter developed a pilot factory in Hue and proved that the concept was viable. Within a year, his factory was producing five tons of desiccated coconut per month and could not meet the growing demand. Unfortunately, as anyone familiar with Vietnam knows, central Vietnam is not known for its supply or quality of coconuts. To supply the factory, coconuts had to be brought from the south along the terribly long and arduous Highway One. This transportation problem made the break-even point and the hope of future profits seem unattainable.

The Ben Tre Plant

> The factory was to be an independent entity owned by the people of Ben Tre...with all profits being reinvested in the factory or distributed as profit sharing to management and labor.

Salter, his IDEVN associates and the Swedish Red Cross agreed to take their model of a successful plant and offer it to the people of Ben Tre, which is in the center of coconut country. A plan was developed to set up a plant, funded by the Swedish Red Cross and IDE contributions of money and equipment, with the know-how supplied by Salter and his team. The factory was to be an independent entity owned by the people of Ben Tre (namely, its workers and management) with all profits being reinvested in the factory or distributed as profit sharing to management and labor, according to a formula.

In recognition of the initial contribution of funding by the Swedish Red Cross, the plan called for a small percentage of the profits to be given to Vietnam's local Red Cross, in perpetuity, as a way to give back to the humanitarian philosophy which launched the venture. To guide the people of Ben Tre in this endeavor and help monitor the performance and profit distribution, a proposal was made for a board of directors with the authority needed to make things happen. That is where I entered the picture.

A Difficult Negotiation

My job was to negotiate with the People's Committee to try to persuade them to accept the Swedish Red Cross/IDE plan of giving them the factory and then structuring and managing it our way. This kind of negotiation would be a routine matter in the United States where I have worked with more American boards than I can remember. However, my only previous negotiations in Vietnam consisted of a project for another NGO which was much smaller and simpler than this one. Hence, my expectations were low and I really did not know what to expect.

The process took three days. Salter, his deputy director/translator and I worked from around 6 or 7 a.m. until late at night in a combination of meetings, negotiations, social functions, strategy sessions and proposal generating. Fortunately, we had our own laptops and printer because the most modern pieces of machinery we saw in the province were typewriters and pencils. Vietnam is still considered Third World, especially in the rural provinces. The process was hindered by many factors, including the lack of knowledge about each other's cultures and customs, the state of uncertainty concerning Vietnam's business laws and, of course, the baggage of mistrust created by years of difficulties between the Vietnamese and foreigners, especially Americans. The necessity of working through translators also added to the difficulty of the task, although I found that my Vietnamese was surprisingly adequate for social functions, which certainly helped with icebreaking.

The process was hindered by many factors, including the lack of knowledge about each other's cultures and customs.

We negotiated in the People's Committee's official meeting room, which seemed to have been designed with maximum formality in mind with a huge table which you nearly had to shout across and a meeting space large enough for well over 100 persons, comfortably seated.

Anyone with experience starting a new venture knows there are many challenges involved, especially in navigating the maze of government-related paperwork. Multiply this by a factor of 10 and you are beginning to understand how the process works in Vietnam. This is not because Vietnamese laws are 10 times more complicated. Rather, it is because no one really knows what the laws are because they are in a state of transition.

The basic flow of the negotiations consisted of each party stating how they wanted the new factory to be organized and managed and by whom. Since it was their country, the cards seemed fairly stacked in the Committee's favor. All I could do was state the desire of the funding agencies to create a factory with the greatest likelihood of success and explain our credentials in establishing small, private enterprises and structuring boards to guide them. Most of our time I spent delivering basic microeconomics, free market and entrepreneurial lectures, combined with examples of highly successful Western enterprises structured along the same models as the one we were proposing. They listened, came around a little to our way of thinking, proposed a few compromises and we went on from there.

Three Key Objectives

There were three key objectives in our strategy. First, we wanted "our" man to be the managing director/CEO. This was obvious to me after interviewing a number of candidates. The choice of manager initially recommended by

IDE and the Swedish Red Cross was far and away the best man for the job. Second, we held out for a Western-style board, with real authority to guide the enterprise. And, third, the enterprise had to be a separate, independent entity, not part of any existing state-owned enterprise. After some effort, we succeeded in putting our plan into place, with the strong support and understanding of our Vietnamese collaborators.

The board consisted of seven members:

- IDE's man, Dan Salter, serving as acting chairman of the board (at least through the start-up phase)
- the newly-appointed managing director (our Vietnamese entrepreneur who was initially rejected by the People's Committee)
- the Vice Chairman of the People's Committee (who is also chairman of the People's Committee for Economy)
- a local state-owned factory manager with experience in the coconut industry and with considerable experience in exporting, which is important once the factory has a surplus product to export
- an elected representative from the factory workers (an idea modeled after participatory management

After some effort, we succeeded in putting our plan into place.

and employee stock ownership philosophies which are easily accepted in socialist economies)
- a member appointed by the Swedish Red Cross funders
- a representative of the local Vietnamese Red Cross, partial beneficiary of the factory's eventual profits

Each of the seven directors would have one equal vote on all matters. We came out of the negotiations feeling very positive and we genuinely believed our Vietnamese counterparts felt the same way.

There were some important lessons in these negotiations. First, the Vietnamese people and leadership are searching for better ways to manage their economy. No leader wants his people to suffer needlessly when a new approach may improve the lives of poor people. While many of our ideas were quite new to our counterparts, they were genuinely interested in listening to them.

Second, working with the Vietnamese takes time. We should not be surprised if Vietnamese officials do not exactly applaud when an American arrives announcing, "I'm here to help you. Trust me!" You need to invest strongly in relationships to get things done there. This means paying attention to little things such as knowing how to use chopsticks and other basic customs before getting invited to a ceremonial dinner.

Third, the results are in the follow-through. Many foreign organizations are now trying to push their way into the Vietnamese market. But success will come first (and best) to those who take a collaborative approach. It is their country. It is their people who are going to do the work, and hopefully be the largest beneficiaries of our projects.

We cannot expect to always do things our way, but we can work together to find out what works and what does not work. I believe that the Vietnamese people will learn that a good board of directors and a participative management style led by a good entrepreneur is one of those things that works in any country.

— *Director's Monthly, Vol. 20, No. 9, September 1996*

Vietnam Update:
The Ben Tre Coconut Project Board Six Months Later

Roger H. Ford, Ph.D.
Zane Showker Professor of Entrepreneurship
James Madison University
Harrisonburg, Virginia

In the last article, I discussed my experiences in 1996 when I had the opportunity to help create a Western-style board of directors for a new desiccated coconut factory in Ben Tre, a province in southern Vietnam. This article updates that report and offers some general thoughts about applying Western board theory in a radically different culture.

In spite of the good intentions of the local Ben Tre authorities to try the western-style experiment in factory organization, ownership and governance, things are not so simple in the Socialist Republic of Vietnam.

While on sabbatical from JMU, I was in Vietnam with my family for nearly six months. While doing an analysis for another project, I was asked to help out on a negotiation between the People's Committee (the local Vietnamese governing body) and the Swedish Red Cross. The Swedish Red Cross had been heavily involved in the Vietnamese coconut industry for many years. It had spent more than

$300,000 on their project over the past three years through its contract agency, IDE International, an American-Canadian non-governmental, nonprofit organization or NGO, engaged in helping the world's poor by providing affordable, appropriate technologies to rural farmers. The crux of the Swedish Red Cross project was to breathe some new life into the Vietnamese coconut industry, including finding new uses and markets for coconuts.

As previously stated, the Vietnamese authorities in Ben Tre province were eager to build a Swedish Red Cross-supported desiccated coconut factory. Following some tough negotiations, they accepted a Western-style board of directors as a condition for continued support by the Swedish Red Cross. In return, the Swedish Red Cross agreed to build the factory, provide equipment, training, start-up funding and oversight until the operation could stand on its own. I ended my last article claiming victory and case closed.

Now, as Paul Harvey says, "Here is the rest of the story." In spite of the good intentions of local Ben Tre authorities to try the Western-style experiment in factory organization, ownership and governance, things are not so simple in the Socialist Republic of Vietnam. The plan for the factory and its board of directors did not quite turn out as anticipated in the first article. Approval of such a radical concept had to go through central authorities in Hanoi and they were not convinced. It was not necessarily that the officials thought we had a bad concept, but rather that Vietnamese business law—embryonic as it is—did not provide a way to implement the entity we proposed. Further, the difficulty of changing the system to accommodate our wishes was simply overwhelming. Therefore, a compromise was proposed and eventually agreed upon.

The project director, Dan Salter, a British expatriate employed by IDE and funded through the Swedish Red Cross grant, and his staff diligently set about persuading the authorities to try the proposed organization and governance model. It appears that local People's Committee members were also supportive of the concept, although in Vietnam, as elsewhere, truth is often hard to discover. However, the bottom line was that the central government in Hanoi said "No." Several other ideas were considered, including a joint venture model and trying to set up the factory as a humanitarian, nonprofit venture. These ideas also went nowhere, but a final compromise was found.

The project director (a British expatriate employed by IDE and funded through the SRC grant) and his staff tried diligently to persuade the authorities to try the proposed organization and governance model.

It was decided to set up the factory as a wholly-owned operation of an existing company in Ben Tre. Fortunately, this company was managed by the project director selected by the Swedish Red Cross team to head their desiccated coconut project. While we initially felt it was in the Managing Director's best interest to have his other duties legally separated from the new plant, in the end, everyone agreed that this compromise was not totally bad. What was lost in independence may have been mitigated by the support structure the existing firm offered. Most importantly, the Vietnamese government agreed. As a compromise to the proposed independent factory with an independent board of directors, the new proposal called for the same group to function as an "advisory board." This point should be interesting to private board members in that *the board originally created in Vietnam was very similar to the boards of private firms in at least one critical way—these boards do not have real power, aside from that earned from knowledge, wisdom, persuasion and results.* The true authority over the desiccated coconut plant now belongs to the three-man governing board which oversees the business, of which the new plant is a part. To the extent that the governing board feels the advisory board is useful, it will continue to exist. However, just like the owner of a private company here in the United States, if the legal authority over the board feels as if the board is not useful or even a hindrance, then the advisory board will disappear. In the interest of moving this humanitarian experiment forward, the Swedish Red Cross was willing to take that risk.

Despite this seemingly large setback, (the funders had, after all, given up absolute control of a project that they had invested years and several hundred thousand dollars on), the experiment still had positive prospects. One bright spot was the reception of the advisory board concept by the managing director, his two outside governing directors and the other advisory board members recruited to fill the team. It was now late May 1996, and I was recruited to help with the project again. This time I was to organize and lead a training workshop for the new advisory board. In addition to the managing director and the other members of the governing board, the workshop was attended by all but one of the proposed advisory board members. At the beginning of the workshop, I sensed some discomfort from nearly all of the board members. It was the first board training class any of them had attended. It was also the first Western-style business training many of them had ever had. The managing director needed to be convinced that the board would help him. Like-

The board originally created in Vietnam is very similar to the boards of private firms in at least one critical way — these boards do not have real power, aside from that earned from knowledge, wisdom, persuasion, and results!

wise, some of the outsiders needed to be convinced that they could really help the venture, and, more importantly, that their contributions would be respected and accepted.

The workshop lasted two days. Of course, it was really equivalent to a one-day workshop, due to the time spent working through an interpreter. However, in the end, Dan Salter, the British expatriate who is serving as Chairman of the Board, our interpreter and I felt we had succeeded. The group seemed enthusiastic about their roles and a team was emerging. The workshop evaluation forms revealed a strong appreciation for the material on how to utilize the Western-style board. The only criticism was that the class was too short and the participants wanted more training!

Immediately following the end of the workshop, the board held its first meeting. I was allowed to observe this meeting and I was very pleased at what I saw. The board members were enthusiastic and pushed through their opening agenda in a professional manner. Most members participated and seemed eager to make their experiment a success.

In the final analysis, success must be measured by more than the initial excitement of the advisory board. The plant must be established and the venture must produce a high quality product at a profit. The advisory board tool is an important factor, and it is now positioned to play a key role in the venture. A lot is riding on this experiment. As a new concept for Vietnam, this project will be closely watched. If the project is deemed a success, it may help usher in more reform in Vietnam, especially with respect to Western-style business approaches. However, if the project fails or does not live up to expectations—reasonable or otherwise—there could be negative repercussions for Vietnam's future willingness to experiment with free market business ideas. Let us all hope that Vietnam's introduction to the board concept will be a great success!

— *Director's Monthly, Vol. 20, No. 11, November 1996*

Chapter Six:
THE BOTTOM LINE -
Evaluating The CEO Of The Private Company

This final chapter deals with a particularly difficult topic. Namely, how directors evaluate their private company CEO when, more than likely, the CEO owns the company. It is one thing for company owners to accept advice and other input from directors on specific issues, challenges and problems. It is quite another matter for those owner/managers to accept feedback on their overall performance as leaders. Now we are getting personal!

Nevertheless, one of the greatest contributions the private company board can make is to give the CEO a comprehensive, detailed performance appraisal covering all relevant areas of his performance as a leader. The company owner suffers from a major handicap - he does not have a boss. This is especially true for more established, highly successful company owners. The start-up, stagnant, or struggling company has many bosses. Bankers, investors, creditors, unhappy customers, disgruntled employees and others serve as surrogates for a "real boss," that is, a boss with the line authority to hire and fire. However, as compa-

nies become more successful, owners can become over-confident, arrogant and even smug about their abilities. They can become isolated from meaningful criticism and feedback, which we all need to keep improving and growing.

The three articles in this chapter were spearheaded by co-author Jerry Schoenfeld, a former colleague from James Madison University. Dr. Schoenfeld is a human resource specialist and his contributions here are greatly appreciated. These articles were originally written and published by Director's Monthly as a series and they are reprinted here with the same intention. Taken together, they describe a step-by-step process for providing a constructive performance appraisal for the company owner CEO.

Evaluating the CEO-Owner:
Process And Criteria

Roger H. Ford, Ph.D.
Zane Showker Professor of Entrepreneurship
James Madison University
Harrisonburg, Virginia

Gerald A. Schoenfeld, Jr., Ph.D.
Associate Professor of Management
Florida Gulf Coast University
Ft. Myers, Florida

Every director knows the benefits of formal appraisal for company employees. Regular review of personnel performance can enhance employee development and motivation, link employee performance to the company's strategic plans, assist succession planning and provide legal documentation for personnel decisions, to name just a few benefits. Yet, there is one employee who can and often does escape formal performance review—the CEO of the privately held company. This article explores why CEO appraisals are so rare in private companies, and how and why they should be conducted.

How can you evaluate someone who not only runs the business, but owns it?

CEO Appraisal: Why Do It?

One of the great paradoxes of performance appraisal is that the higher you are on the organizational chart, the less likely you will be formally evaluated and given quality feedback on your performance. This state of affairs is reinforced by the myth that CEOs neither want or need to have their performance formally evaluated. CEOs typically are confident, self-reliant, self-directed, and tolerant of ambiguity. Additionally, an argument can be made that the CEO's performance is that of the organization, so the CEO and his board can assess his performance based on organizational performance indicators.

However, a compelling argument can be made that every CEO needs to have a regular formal appraisal of his or her performance. Everyone, including the CEO, has developmental needs. Yet, research has found that CEOs, partially due to their self-confidence and career success, are reluctant to acknowledge their limitations. Moreover, senior managers and directors often are loath to offer developmental feedback in an informal manner. Not appraising the CEO can even have a trickle-down effect for the entire organization. Studies have shown that it is easier to give effective appraisals when one receives effective appraisals, which means the ability of CEOs to accurately evaluate the managers reporting to them depends on whether the CEO receives appraisals. Finally, formal appraisal may be a vehicle for the board to assist the CEO in becoming more adept at thinking strategically, communicating to others and exercising leadership.

Developing a Process

One of the first considerations for CEO appraisal is how to set up an effective system for evaluation. The first and most important step is to have genuine support from the board of directors and CEO-owner regarding the need and value of appraisal. Without the support of the key parties involved, any appraisal system is doomed for failure at the onset.

> **Formal appraisal may be a vehicle for the board to assist the CEO in becoming more adept at thinking strategically, communicating to others and exercising leadership.**

A formal appraisal process will evaluate the CEO on a set list of relevant performance variables or dimensions. Informal evaluations are those where one or more board members individually or jointly provide opinions on how the CEO is performing. These opinions, whether solicited or not by the CEO, can provide valuable information to the CEO on his performance. But this should be done in addition to, not in place of, a formal evaluation process.

Another key to implementing a formal appraisal process is to evaluate performance on a regular basis. Typically, this can correspond with the firm's fiscal year, but depending on the volatility of your organization's environment, a shorter or longer appraisal time cycle may be more relevant for your needs.

Types of Performance Appraisals

There are a wide assortment of methods for appraising performance. One technique that has been used since the 1920s, and which is the most popular today, is called the graphic rating scale (GRS). The GRS focuses on key performance dimensions, which often take the form of traits (e.g., vision, integrity, leadership) chosen by the organization, depending on its needs and specific job characteristics. Evaluation of the dimensions is made by using anchored rating scales (e.g., 1=unsatisfactory to 5=outstanding). This approach for evaluation performance is attractive for the CEO position because it affords easy customization to the firm's unique situation, it is relatively easy to use and understand, it is quick to complete, and it has great intuitive appeal. A key to the success of this appraisal approach is that each performance dimension must be clearly and specifically defined and ratings should be supported as much as possible with actual instances of good or poor performance if the appraisal is going to generate developmental feedback for the CEO.

Many other techniques for appraising performance do exist and each approach brings its own strengths and advantages. A good source for more information on various performance appraisal methods is "Increasing Productivity Through Performance Appraisal" by Gary Latham and Kenneth Wexley (New York: Addison Wesley Publishing Company, 1994). One important point to remember in choosing a performance appraisal method is that it must be useful for your purposes, as well as flexible and broad enough to be relevant for the CEO position.

> **One important point to remember in choosing a performance appraisal method is that it must be useful for your purposes, and flexible as well as broad enough to be relevant for the CEO position.**

CEO Dimensions to Evaluate

A key issue in appraising the CEO is determining what performance dimensions should be used. One excuse for not evaluating CEOs is that their job is just too broad to allow accurate and relevant evaluation. However, for most firms, there are consistent performance areas that are particularly important for the CEO. Acknowledging that every firm is different and that the performance evaluation should be customized to your unique needs, the following performance dimensions are typically closely aligned with the roles and responsibilities of the CEO-owner.

- *Strategic management.* Creates and promotes a vision and direction for the firm. Formulates and implements a strategy fitted to the firm's internal and external environment and key stakeholders. Achieves desired goals and objectives on a set timetable. Allocates resources efficiently and consistently with strategic objectives.

- *Financial planning.* Sets and pursues short-term and long-term financial goals. Prudently utilizes appropriate financial controls to manage operations and protect risks. Takes risks where appropriate for long-term firm profitability.

CEO Dimensions to Evaluate:
- ✓ **Strategic management**
- ✓ **Financial planning**
- ✓ **Personnel management**
- ✓ **Customer relations**
- ✓ **Leadership**
- ✓ **Communications**
- ✓ **New product planning and development**
- ✓ **Board relations**

- *Personnel management.* Creates in all employees an awareness that their best effort is essential and that they will share in the rewards of the firm's success. Develops and maintains an effective top management team capable of achieving strategic objectives. Provides for management succession. Ensures a work environment that is in compliance with equal employment opportunity laws.

- *Customer relations.* Stays in close contact with customer needs and desires. Emphasizes customer service throughout the organization. Anticipates changes in customer demographics. Seeks new customer bases.

- *Leadership.* Establishes key values and philosophies to guide employee behavior. Ensures that firm operations are appropriately managed on a continuing basis. Is fair and impartial in decision-making and employee interactions. Is perceived by others, both inside and outside the organization, as an effective leader.

- *Communications.* Facilitates and reinforces effective communication between departments and work units. Informs employees of firm mission and strategic objections. Explains changes in procedures and policies in a timely and effective manner. Serves as a spokesperson for the firm to external stakeholders.

> **Other areas that should be considered include market analysis, labor relations, production and manufacturing, integrity, firm culture, quality and community involvement, to name just a few.**

- *New product planning and development.* Emphasizes innovation as a key to future growth and firm success. Invests resources for the creation and development of long-term projects. Seeks to exceed customer expectations. Pursues competitive advantage through development of product and service innovations.

- *Board relations.* Develops and recommends to the board strategic and business plans. Formulates budgets acceptable to the board. Communicates effectively with board members keeping them fully informed on relevant firm issues and activities. Maintains positive professional relationships with each director.

This list of dimensions is not meant to be exhaustive, rather it represents common performance responsibilities we have found in dealing with private firm CEOs. Other areas that should be considered include market analysis, labor relations, production and manufacturing, integrity, firm culture, quality and community involvement, to name just a few.

While defining the performance dimension is essential, the definitions given above are examples that should be customized to your specific CEO and work environment. Different organizations may also choose to give subjective weights to the various performance dimensions based on relevance and criticality to their own work setting.

— *Director's Monthly, Vol. 20, No. 3, March 1996*

Evaluating the CEO-Owner:
Who Should Do The Job?

Roger H. Ford, Ph.D.
Zane Showker Professor of Entrepreneurship
James Madison University
Harrisonburg, Virginia

Gerald A. Schoenfeld, Jr., Ph.D.
Associate Professor of Management
Florida Gulf Coast University
Ft. Myers, Florida

In our last article, we set forth why and how CEO-owners should be evaluated, but we reserved the most important question for this article: Who should do the evaluating?

No single individual can provide a complete and accurate review of all the responsibilities and activities of a CEO.

Obviously, no single individual can provide a complete and accurate review of all the responsibilities and activities of a CEO. Nor can a single group—not even the board of directors. Boards should gather input from multiple stakeholders, including immediate subordinates, fellow CEOs who have contact with your CEO, key individuals in other agencies (e.g., suppliers, customers), community leaders and even a self-evaluation from the CEO. The evaluations from each of these important stakeholders should then be combined to create an overall performance appraisal.

Advantages

Using multiple evaluators offers at least three distinct advantages. First, it ensures perspective, as raters will be looking at the CEO from differing vantage points. Second, it encourages honesty, because the more raters there are, the easier it is to preserve anonymity. Finally, it fosters objectivity, since many of the raters have inequitable power relationships with the CEO. As an old French saying goes, "No man is a hero to his valet."* By the same token, no CEO is a hero to his direct report (or a heroine to hers). Assured anonymity, a CEO's subordinate may offer valuable insights into a leader's weak points as well as his strengths.

For the CEO performance appraisal process to succeed, it should be managed by individuals respected by the CEO. The individuals should be selected by the board, not the CEO, although the CEO should have input into and, in some cases, veto power over the decision.

The top appraiser can be a peer, a professional or a combination of the two. The peer appraiser will be a CEO or director who may or may not serve on the board. The "professional" appraiser will be a human resources specialist, either an employee or an outside consultant.

Attributed to French salon pundit Madame Cornuel (1605-1695).

Top Evaluators

Ideally, the two types of evaluators will work jointly. For example, a board member may wish to team up with an outside consultant, or a CEO who is not on the board may rely on the personnel expertise of the company's human relations staff. The important thing is to ensure that the top evaluator (or one of the two) is independent from the CEO. In no case should an employee have sole responsibility for directing the CEO's evaluation.

The top evaluator(s), once chosen, will have their work cut out for them. They will set up an appraisal system and create or approve an evaluation form. They should then identify relevant raters and give them forms to fill out with a deadline for completing them. Finally, the top evaluator should synthesize all relevant input into one final appraisal and communicate the results to the CEO. Our next article will explore this sensitive mission.

— *Director's Monthly, Vol. 20, No. 5, May 1996*

Evaluating The CEO-Owner:
How To Minimize The Impact Of Politics

Roger H. Ford, Ph.D.
Zane Showker Professor of Entrepreneurship
James Madison University
Harrisonburg, Virginia

Gerald A. Schoenfeld, Jr., Ph.D.
Associate Professor of Management
Florida Gulf Coast University
Ft. Myers, Florida

When evaluating at the top of the organization, politics are inevitable. Appraisals become more political the higher one rises in an organization. In part, this is because CEOs often operate without a formal job description, and even when these are written up, they are often imprecise and broad or even inaccurate. This is especially true when the entrepreneurial founder of the firm is still at the helm or even when control has been passed to descendants.

CEO appraisal can benefit both the company and its leader.

To minimize the impact of politics on appraisals, boards should:
- have a well-written job description for the CEO
- create clear and specific job expectations annually

- train raters on how to complete the evaluation form
- use multiple raters, thereby limiting the impact of any one individual's political agenda
- create a culture both in the company and in the boardroom, that reinforces the importance and value of performance appraisals.

To minimize the impact of politics:
- **have a well-written job description for the CEO**
- **create clear and specific job expectations annually**
- **train raters on how to complete the evaluation form**
- **use multiple raters, thereby limiting the impact of any one individual's political agenda**
- **create a culture that reinforces the importance and value of performance appraisals.**

Building Acceptance

When directors anticipate that the CEO-owner will be less than enthusiastic about the idea of being evaluated, they may find increased acceptance by utilizing a respected, neutral third party and by including self-appraisal information by the CEO-owner.

Directors also can build support for the idea of CEO appraisal incrementally over a period of months by following a logical plan. For example, a board may begin by discussing the objectives of evaluation (e.g., to link CEO and company performance) and then move on to discuss the benefits of achieving these objectives (e.g., greater profit-

Evaluating The CEO-Owner: Minimize The Impact Of Politics

ability for the company and hence higher satisfaction and pay for the CEO). Once these discussions have taken place, the board can delve into the particulars of the evaluation process itself.

The board should initiate discussion of CEO-owner appraisal at a time when its importance and relevance is readily apparent, such as when the board is engaging in strategic and/or succession planning.

Providing Feedback

The most difficult, yet most important, aspect of the performance appraisal is providing performance feedback to the CEO. This task is especially difficult for private boards, where one serves at the request of the CEO.

> **The board should initiate discussion of CEO/owner appraisal at a time when its importance and relevance is readily apparent, such as when the board is engaging in strategic and/or succession planning.**

When delivering performance appraisal results to the CEO, the board should select a person (ideally someone on the board) who has experience giving performance feedback, strong interpersonal skills and perhaps most importantly, the respect of the CEO. The feedback giver/board member should take control of the meeting from the onset by stating the purpose and importance of the meeting and setting a clear agenda to be followed.

Strengths First

To gain the CEO's receptivity to hearing developmental information, it is a good idea to make the feedback discussion participative. One way to facilitate dialogue is to begin by focusing on those areas that can be considered performance *strengths,* as rated on the appraisal form. By focusing on superior performance areas at the onset of the performance discussion, the appraisal receiver will be more willing to acknowledge and discuss performance weaknesses later in the feedback session.

To get into weaknesses, the feedback giver can ask the CEO if there are any work performance areas he or she would like to discuss as areas needing improvement. Chances are, the CEO will bring up areas the board has (or should have) already identified as trouble spots. The feedback session should always conclude on a positive note, with an agreed upon set of performance and developmental goals and specific follow-up dates.

Conclusion

Regular, formal evaluation of the CEO should be an important activity for all boards of directors. If you do not have a CEO evaluation system currently in place, then start exploring the creation of one today.

— *Director's Monthly, Volume 20, No. 7, July 1996*

Chapter Seven:
SUMMARY

This book has attempted to introduce the subject of using boards of directors for privately-owned companies. Unlike their larger, publicly-owned counterparts, private companies have no real compulsion or incentive to utilize a board, other than the belief that a board will provide a net benefit to their firms. That is, the owners of private companies will only use boards when they believe that they will be the beneficiaries of these boards.

I cannot promise that every private board will benefit from a board of directors. Indeed, I have elsewhere reported extensive research results which suggest that in some cases, outside boards may actually hinder entrepreneurial performance. However, it remains my conviction that in most cases, private company performance can indeed be improved over time with a properly constructed and intelligently managed board of directors. The board is not a quick-fix tool and therein often lies the debate about board effectiveness. Those who are disappointed with their boards are often those managers who gave up after only a brief or half hearted attempt at board leadership.

Free enterprise dictates that the ultimate choice belongs to the owners and managers of each firm. The laboratory experience of every private firm will be the final place where private company boards must be evaluated. I have offered my views. Now, you must decide. I leave you with one final observation—a bit of ancient wisdom, which needs no commentary:

> "Plans fail for lack of counsel,
> but with many advisors
> they succeed."

Proverbs 15:22, Holy Bible, New International Version

Contributing Authors

Warren L. Braun

Warren L. Braun, P.E., is the founder and Chairman of the Board of ComSonics, a Harrisonburg, Virginia company in the cable television industry. Braun, a true entrepreneur, has guided ComSonics from its beginnings as a consulting engineering firm, through business expansion, entry into the *Fortune* 500 and transformation into an Employee Stock Ownership Plan (ESOP). His insights into the role of the board at various stages of private company ownership are based on his solid experience and deep theoretical knowledge. Braun holds various degrees and awards, including an honorary doctorate from Shenandoah University. He has authored numerous articles and books. He resides in Harrisonburg with his wife Lillian (Dickie). They have a grown daughter and one grandson.

S. Michael Camp

S. Michael Camp, Ph.D., is the Director of the National Center for Entrepreneurial Research of the Kauffman Foundation, Kansas City, Missouri. From 1995-1997 he was an Assistant Professor of Strategic Management and Entrepreneurship at James Madison University. Previously,

Camp served as Vice President of Finance and Administration for Creative Control Designs, a manufacturer of computerized digital control systems in Columbus, Ohio.

Gerald A. Schoenfeld, Jr.

Gerald A. Schoenfeld, Jr., Ph.D., is an Associate Professor of Management at Florida Gulf Coast University. He previously served as an Associate Professor of Management at James Madison University until 1997. He has authored numerous academic and practitioner articles in the area of performance appraisal and has presented his work at many professional conferences and meetings. Schoenfeld also consults a wide array of businesses on achieving greater effectiveness from performance appraisal systems.

Stanley C. Vance

Stanley C. Vance, Ph.D., is a long-time friend of the National Association of Corporate Directors (NACD). Presenting Dr. Vance in this book is especially meaningful for me. Vance's pioneering research into the subject of boards of directors inspired my own Ph.D. research and ultimately, my career as a small business management educator.

In 1955, and again in 1964 and 1983, Dr. Vance conducted in-depth studies on boards of major industrial corporations. When I began conducting my own board studies in 1984, Vance's work was considered essential to anyone wishing to understand the role of boards in corporate governance. Well over a decade later, this is still true.

Vance is the William B. Stokely Professor Emeritus in the Department of Management at the University of Tennessee. Throughout his long and distinguished career, he has authored several books and numerous articles on management-related topics. He also served as President of the Academy of Management, among other professional accomplishments.

Marion M. White

Marion M. White, Ph.D., is Associate Professor of Management at James Madison University, where she teaches classes in International Management and Strategic Management. Her research interests include cross-cultural management issues, particularly the effects of culture on perceptions of justice. In addition to her academic credentials, White has extensive work experience in Europe and in the Middle East.

Karen W. Wigginton

Karen W. Wigginton, Ed.D., is Director of the Small Business Development Center and the Student Business Counselor Institute at James Madison University. She teaches courses in Small and Family Business Management and Small Business Consulting. Wigginton is very active in local, state and national organizations and associations which support the role of higher education in economic and entrepreneurial development. She has served on several boards of directors and governmental advisory panels.

References

Alderfer, Clayton P. (1988). Understanding and Consulting to Family Business Boards. Family Business Review. 1, (3), 249-260.

Alexander, J.A. Fennel, M.L. & Halpern, M.T. (1993). Leadership Instability in Hospitals: The Influence of Board-CEO Relations and Organizational Growth and Decline. Administrative Science Quarterly, 38, 74-99.

Andrews, Kenneth R. (1986). Director's Responsibility for Corporate Strategy. Strategic Planning, Pfeiffer, J. William, Editor. University Associates, San Diego, California. 57-69.

Bacon, J., Brown, J.K. (1977). The Board of Directors: Perspectives and Practices in Nine Countries. Academy of Management Journal. 33, (1).

Bank Director's Responsibilities. (1987). Division of Research and Structure. Bureau of Financial Institutions State Corporation Commission. Richmond, Virginia.

Barnard, Chester I. (1976). The Functions of the Executive. Cambridge: Harvard University Press.

Birch, David L. (1987). Job Creation in America. New York: The Free Press.

"A Board Of Directors Extends A Firm's Reach." (1990). Nation's Business, June, 10-12.

Boeker, W. & Goodstein, J. (1993). Performance and Successor Choice: The Moderating Effects of Governance and Ownership. Academy of Management Journal. 36, 172-186.

Bogart, D.B. (1994). Liability of Directors of Chapter 11 Debtors in Possession: "Don't Look Back—Something May Be Gaining On You." American Bankruptcy Law Journal. 68, (Winter) 155-267.

Brown, Buck. (1989) Enterprise. Latest Board Advice is Keep It in the Family. The Wall Street Journal. January, B-1.

Cabot, Louis W. (1976). On an Effective Board. Harvard Business Review. 57, (3).

Castaldi, Richard, and Wortman, Max S., Jr. (1984). Boards of Directors in Small Corporations: An Untapped Resource. American Journal of Small Business. 9, (2), 1-10.

Chandler, Alfred D. Jr. (1978). Strategy and Structure: Chapters in the History of the American Industrial Enterprise. Cambridge: The M.I.T. Press.

Cochran, Philip L.; Wood, Robert A., and Jones, Thomas B. (1985). The Composition of Boards of Directors and the Incidence of Golden Parachutes. Academy of Management Journal. 28, (3), 664-671.

Daily, C.M. & Dalton, D.R. (1993). The Relationship Between Board Composition and Leadership Structure and Bankruptcy Reorganization Outcomes. Journal of Management. 21, 1041-1056.

Daily, C.M. & Dalton, D.R. (1993). Board of Directors Leadership and Structure: Control and Performance Implications. Entrepreneurship Theory and Practice. 17, (3), 65-81.

Danco, Leon A. (1975). It's Your Business - Perpetuate or Liquidate. Retail Control. 44, 48-51.

Danco, Leon A. "Do Boards of Directors Really Help Small Businesses?" *Small Business Forum*, Winter 1991,1992, 9 (3), 88-90.

Danco, Leon A. and Jonovic, Donald J. (1981). Outside Directors in the Family-Owned Business. Cleveland, Ohio: University Press, Inc.

Dooley, Michael, P. (1990). A Practical Guide For The Corporate Director. KPMG Peat Marwick.

Drexler, John A. and Nielsen, James F. (1988). Corporate Leadership: Boards, Directors, and Strategy. Family Business Review. I, (3), 330-333.

Drucker, Peter E. (1989). What Business Can Learn from Nonprofits. Harvard Business Review. July-August. 67, (4). 88-93.

Ford, Roger H. (1989). Establishing and Managing Boards of Directors: The Other View. Family Business Review. II, (2), 142-146.

Ford, Roger H. (1986). Outside Directors and the Privately-Owned Firm: A Study of the *Inc.* 500. Dissertation of Syracuse University.

Ford, Roger H. (1988). Outside Directors and the Privately-Owned Firm: Are They Necessary? Entrepreneurship: Theory and Practice. 13, (1), 49-57.

Ford, Roger H. (1989a). For Many Family Firms, Outside Directors Are a Hindrance Because They Don't Know the Business. The BusinessWeek Newsletter for Family Owned Business. 1, (6), 6.

Ford, Roger H. (1989b). The Board of Directors: A Tool For The Future. Women Owned Businesses, Hagan, Oliver; Rivchun, Carol; Sexton, Donald, Editors. 1989. 79-101. Praeger, New York.

Ford, Roger H. (1987). The Value of Outside Directors: Myth or Reality? Business. 37,(4), 44-48.

Ford, Roger H. *Boards of Directors and the Privately Owned Firm*. Quorum Books, 1992.

Ford, Roger H. "The Sad Truth is—for the Most Part—Boards Do Not Help," *Small Business Forum*, Winter 1991/1992, 9 (3), 91-93.

Ford, Roger H. "Establishing and Managing Boards of Directors: The Other View," *Family Business Review*, 1989, *2 (2)*, 142-146.

Ford, Roger H., and Priesmyer, H. Richard. (1990). Perceptions of Board Influence in *Inc.* 500 Firms: A Comparison of Inside and Outside Boards. Journal of Management in Practice. 2, (1), 37-41.

Ford, Roger H. "The Sad Truth is — for the Most Part — Boards Do Not Help" *Small Business Forum,* 9 (3), pp. 91-93, Winter 1991/1992.

References

Gales, L.M. & Kesner, I.F. (1994). An Analysis of Board of Director Size and Composition in Bankrupt Organizations. Journal of Business Research, 30: 27-39.

Giardina, James A., and Tilghman, Thomas S. (1988). Organization & Compensation of Boards of Directors. Arthur Young: New York, New York.

Harris, Thomas B. (1989). Some Comments on Family Firm Boards. Family Business Review. II, (2), 150-152.

Heidrick, Gardner W. (1984a). Building a Stronger Board. The President. 20, (3), 4-5.

Heidrick, Gardner W. (1984b). An Attractive Alternative: The Board of Advisors. The President. 20, (3), 5.

Heidrick, Gardner W. (1988). Selecting Outside Directors. Family Business Review. 1, (3), 271-277.

The *Inc.* 500. (1984). Inc. December, 136.

Jacobs, Stanford L. (1985). A Well-Chosen Outside Board Gives Owners Peace of Mind. The Wall Street Journal. January 21, 25.

Johnson, Daily and Ellstrand, (1996). Board of Directors. Journal of Management, 22, (3), 433-438.

Johnson, Elmer W. (1990). An Insider's Call for Outside Direction. Harvard Business Review. 68, (2), 46-55.

Judge, W.Q. & Dobbins, G.H. (1995). Antecedents and Effects of Outside Directors Awareness of CEO Decision Style. Journal of Management, (21): 43-46.

Kesner, I.F., and Victor, B., Lamont, B.T. (1986). Board Composition and the Commission of Illegal Acts: An Investigation of the Fortune 500 Companies. Academy of Management Journal. 29, (4), 789.

Lovdal, Michael; Vauer, Raymond A.; and Treverton, Nancy H. (1977). Public Responsibility Committees. Harvard Business Review. May-June.

Lowrie, Roy W., Jr. (1988). Serving God on the Christian School Board. Association of Christian Schools, International, Whittier, California.

Lowrie, Roy W. Jr. (1985). Insights for Chrstian School Board Members. Association of Christian Schools, International, Whittier, CA.

Mace, Myles L. (1971). Directors: Myth and Reality. Boston: Harvard University.

Mathile, Clayton L. (1988). A Business Owner's Perspective on Outside Boards. Family Business Review. 1, (3), 231-237.

Maturi, Richard J. (1989). Small-Business Boardroom. Entrepreneur. 17, (8), 128-132.

Mautz, R. K., and Neumann, F. L. (1970). The Effective Corporate Audit Committee. Harvard Business Review. Boards of Directors: Part I. 83-91.

McCarthy, Charles, Jr., (1989). The Chronicling of Corporate Minutes. Board Practices Monograph. II, (3). 1-4. National Association of Corporate Directors. 1707 L Street, N.W., Washington, D.C. 20036.

Mintzberg, Henry. (1983). Power in and Around Organizations. Englewood Cliffs, New Jersey: Prentice-Hall, Inc.

Moskowitz, Daniel B. (1990). CEOs Laud Outside Directors, But Only If They Are Used Right. The BusinessWeek Newsletter for Family-Owned Business. 2, (11), 1 & 10.

Mueller, Robert Kirk. (1984). Behind the Boardroom Door. New York: Crown Publishers, Inc.

Mueller, Robert Kirk. (1988). Differential Directorship: Special Sensitivities and Roles for Serving the Family Business Board. Family Business Review. 1, (3), 239-247.

Mueller, Robert Kirk. (1990). The Director's & Officer's Guide to Advisory Boards. Westport, Connecticut: Quorum Books.

Nash, John M. (1988). Boards of Privately Held Companies: Their Responsibilities and Structure. Family Business Review. 1, (3), 263-269.

Nash, John M. (1990). Board Tenure. Board Practices, Monograph. National Association of Corporate Directors, 1707 L St., N.W., Suite 560, Washington, D.C. 20036.

Nelson, G. W. (1987). Information Needs of Female Entrepreneurs. Journal of Small Business Management. July, 38-44.

Pfeffer, Jeffrey. (1972). Size and Composition of Boards of Directors: The Organization and Its Environment. Administrative Science Quarterly. 2, 218-228.

Phillips, Bruce D. (1989). Small Business Administration. Personal telephone interview with the author on November 3, 1989.

Pocket Guide for Directors and Guidelines for Financial Institution Directors. (1988). Federal Deposit Insurance Corporation, Washington, D.C.

Posner, Bruce G. (1983). A Board Even an Entrepreneur Could Love. Inc. April, 73-87.

Revchun, Carol; Hagan, Oliver L.; and Sexton, Donald L. (1989). Your Board of Directors: A Tool for the Future. The Woman Entrepreneur: Reflections on the Future. Praeger Publishing, New York.

Robinson, Richard B, Jr., (1982). The Importance of "Outsiders" in Small Firm Strategic Planning. Academy Of Management Journal. 25, (1), 80-93.

Say, Jean Baptiste. (1816). Catechism of Political Economy. London, Sherwood, 28-29.

Schipani, Cindy, A. and Siedel, George J. (1988). Legal Liability: The Board of Directors. Family Business Review. 1, (3), 279-285.

Sherman, S. P. (1988). Pushing Corporate Boards To Be Better. Fortune. July, 58-67.

Swoboda, Frank. (1990). Empowering the Rank and File. The Washington Post. Sunday, September 30, 1990. H3.

References

The Job Nobody Wants. (1986). Business Week. 57-61.

The State of Small Business. (1989). A Report Of The President. United States Government Printing Office. Washington.

Tillman, Fred A. (1988). Commentary on Legal Liability: Organizing the Advisory Council. Family Business Review. 1, (3), 287-288.

Twiss, Brian C. (1980). Managing Technological Innovation. London: Longman.

Vance, Stanley C. (1964). Boards of Directors: Structure and Performance. Eugene, Oregon: University of Oregon Press.

Vance, Stanley C. (1983). Corporate Leadership: Boards, Directors, and Strategy. New York: McGraw-Hill.

Vance, Stanley C. (1955). Functional Directors and Corporate Performance. Business Week. November 26, 128-130.

Vance, Stanley C. (1955). "Functional Directors and Corporate Performance." *Business Week,* November 26, 128-30.

Vance Stanley. *Boards of Directors: Structure and Performance.* Eugene. Oregon: University of Oregon Press, 1964.

Verschoor, Curtis C. (1989). Building A More Effective Audit Committee. Board Practices Monograph. II, (4), 1-20.

Wallen, Eileen. (1989). ESOPS May Be A Good Way To Keep the Company in the Family. The BusinessWeek Newsletter for Family-Owned Business. 1, (13), 1.

Ward, John L. *Creating Effective Boards for Private Enterprises.* Jossey-Bass Inc., Publishers, 1991.

Ward, John L. (1988). The Active Board With Outside Directors and the Family Firm. Family Business Review. 1, (3), 223-229.

Ward, John L. and Handy, James L. (1988) A Survey of Board Practices. Family Business Review. 1, (3), 289-308.

Ward, John L. (1989). Defining and Researching Inside Versus Outside Directors: A Rebuttal to the Rebuttal. Family Business Review. II, (2), 147-150.

Wasnak, Lynn. (1989). Helping Hands. Ohio Business. 13, (4), 21-25.

Westphal, J.D. & Zajac, E.J. (1995). Who Shall Govern? CEO/Board Power, Demographic Similarity, and New Director Selection. Administrative Science Quarterly. (40): 60-83.

Whisler, Thomas L. (1988). The Role of the Board in the Threshold Firm. Family Business Review. 1, (3), 309-321.

Who Needs Outside Directors? (1989). Strategic Direction. (44). 27-28.

Williams, Roy O. (1989). How to Get Family Members Interested in the Business - And to Want to Run It. The BusinessWeek Newsletter for Family Owned Business. 1 (9), 7.

Wollner, Kenneth S. (1991). Preparing for Changes in the Directors and Officers Liability Insurance Market. Director's Monthly. 15, (1), 10-11.

Wommack, William W. (1979). The Board's Most Important Function. Harvard

Business Review. September-October.

Wood, Robert W. (1989). A Primer on the Ins and Outs of ESOPs: How to Decide If It's the Right Option for Your Firm. The BusinessWeek Newsletter for Family Owned Business. 1. (25), 9.

Zahra, Shaker A. and Pearce, John A. II. (1989). Boards of Directors and Corporate Financial Performance: A Review and Integrative Model. Journal of Management. 15, (2), 291-334.